NIGHT FLYING WOMAN

NIGHT FLYING WOMAN

An Ojibway Narrative

By IGNATIA BROKER

Illustrated by
STEVEN PREMO

With a Foreword by
PAULETTE FAIRBANKS MOLIN

MINNESOTA HISTORICAL SOCIETY PRESS
ST. PAUL · 1983

LIBRARY OF CONGRESS CATALOGING IN PUBLICATION DATA
Broker, Ignatia.
    Night Flying Woman.

    (Publications of the Minnesota Historical Society)
    Summary: In the accounts of the lives of several
generations of Ojibway people in Minnesota is much
information about their history and culture.
    1. Chippewa Indians--Social life and customs.
2. Chippewa Indians--History. [1. Chippewa Indians--
Social life and customs. 2. Chippewa Indians--History.
3. Indians of North America--Social life and customs.
4. Indians of North America--History] I. Premo,
Steven, ill. II. Title. III. Series.
E99.C6B79   1983   306'.08997   83-13360

Dedication

*To those Indian people who organized,
incorporated, and built the Indian social groups,
drum and dance groups, help and care groups, and
educational groups, to those of the activist
and conservative groups, I dedicate this book.*

Contents

Foreword

NIGHT FLYING WOMAN is a story in the tradition of
the Ojibway people. It is also the story of culture
contact with strangers, contact that drastically altered an ancient way of life. In *Night Flying Woman*
we meet several generations of one family group;
through their lives we learn the traditions, beliefs,
customs, and some history of the Ojibway in Minnesota. We follow Ni-bo-wi-se-gwe – Night Flying
Woman, or Oona – from her birth during an eclipse
of the sun to her old age; her experiences, memories,
and dreams speak of the changes that beset her people. In her development we see the traditional cycle
of the Ojibway from the naming ceremony to the
role of elders as teachers.

The Ojibway are known in their own language as
Anishinabe, original people. Their language and culture are based on an oral tradition; hence the importance of memory, listening, and speaking. "Listen,
and you will hear the patterns of life," young Oona
learned. Children at an early age also were taught
the importance of listening to the Old Ones; for, as
the contemporary storyteller informs her grandchildren: "It has always been the custom for us to tell

ix

what must be passed on so that our ways will be known to the Ojibway children of the future."

Although Ni-bo-wi-se-gwe lived centuries after her people originally moved westward from the Atlantic coast, she knew their past. In her own story other, later journeys unfolded, as she and her family tried to avoid contact with the ever increasing numbers of voyageurs and other strangers in their land. Her family's migration ended when its members were removed by treaty to the White Earth Reservation in northwestern Minnesota.

Culture contact changed an entire way of life, as treaty makers, missionaries, fur traders, and lumber companies, all acting in their own interests, altered the land and manipulated the Indian people. In the 1800s a series of treaties confined the Ojibway to reservations, thereby opening up large areas of land to white settlers. As more and more land seekers moved in, succeeding treaties reduced reservation boundaries. The General Allotment Act of 1887 further eroded the land base, not only for the Ojibway, but for other tribal groups across the country. This legislation, also known as the Dawes Act, was intended to "civilize" the Indians who were to become farmers, although what land was left them often had little or no farming potential. The Dawes Act along with the Nelson Act of 1889 and the Clapp Act of 1906 enabled the timber industry to take over much of Minnesota's woodlands.

White Earth Reservation, established by treaty in 1867, was planned by the government to be the only Ojibway reservation in Minnesota — a plan that ultimately failed. The first group of Ojibway people

was moved there in the spring of 1868. According to
Julia Spears, an early resident, "They named their
new home Gah-wah-bah-bi-gon-i-kah, or White
Earth, from the white clay found under the black
soil." Many descriptions attest to the area's beauty
and abundance. An early account, for example,
stated: "The region was dotted with lakes. Game
and fish were plentiful. Immense wild rice beds were
annually harvested and large areas of sugar bush
provided an additional abundant food supply." As
the account also pointed out, however, to the white
settlers spread along the borders of the reservation,
"it seemed absurd that less than 2,000 people should
occupy 800,000 acres of land of so great value both
for agriculture and for standing pine." In a series of
legislative and administrative acts, "the virtual
mutilation . . . of the White Earth Reservation was
soon effected," as tribally held pinelands were allotted to individual members.[1]

Describing the impact of the Clapp Act, which
permitted adult mixed-blood Ojibway of the White
Earth Reservation to sell their lands, Now-ah-quay-
gi-shig, Pine Point school superintendent from 1903
to 1911, stated that it "brought both grief and happiness to many people." Land buyers approached
Ojibway people who did not know about the act,
and witnesses were easily procured to "subscribe to
affadavits that the Indian in question had white
blood in his veins and in many cases the white blood

[1] Spears, "History of White Earth," and E. L. Lawson, "The
Rise and Fall of an Indian Forest Community," in Gerald R.
Vizenor, comp. and ed., *Escorts to White Earth: 100 Year Reserva-
tion, 1868-1968*, 110, 112, 144 (Minneapolis, 1968).

ran through the branches of the family tree for many generations to some remote Canadian Frenchman." Now-ah-quay-gi-shig concluded his account of this "very unfortunate piece of legislation" with the following incident: "The writer remembers a case where the land man had some difficulty in establishing white blood in the Indian whom he sought to deal with and he came to the writer and the writer suggested that he try and trace the Indian's ancestry to Adam."[2]

All Minnesota Ojibway reservations except Red Lake were eventually allotted; Red Lake, consequently, is the only one that is not checkered with tracts owned by non-Indians. Before the allotment policy ended in the 1930s, two-thirds of the Indian land in the United States had passed into white hands. The effects on the White Earth Reservation were devastating. By 1971, only 4 per cent of the original reservation was Indian-owned trust land; another 4 per cent was "marginal land" purchased for the Indians under the New Deal's Farm Security Administration program. The fragmentation of Indian holdings created severe obstacles to tribal land use, including problems of jurisdiction, economic development, and heirship.[3]

The lumber industry, as this book depicts, had an enormous impact on the land and people of White Earth. Just the timber north of Pine Point kept one

[2] Now-ah-quay-gi-shig (N. B. Hurr), "The Clapp Act," in Benno Watrin, comp., *The Ponsfordian, 1880-1930: A Collection of Historical Data Dealing Especially with Pioneer Days of Ponsford, Becker County, Minnesota*, 34, 43 (Park Rapids, 1930).
[3] League of Women Voters of Minnesota, *Indians in Minnesota*, 14, 31 (St. Paul, 1971).

large lumber company in constant operation winter
and summer for about fifteen years.[4] Ni-bo-wi-se-
gwe's dream of an Indian standing on a log with
many blurred white faces behind him was realized.
Until the forests were stripped, the logging industry
accounted for many of the changes in the lives of
these Ojibway people.

Night Flying Woman is a legacy for the young, for the
children who "could hum the songs from the radio
but did not know the songs of the drum." It
describes a philosophy of living that is as essential
and meaningful today as it was in the past. One of
the tenets is sharing, a value that sustains many contemporary Ojibway people in crowded, modern-day
apartments in urban environments. Another tenet is
respect—for the earth, for plant and animal life, and
for one another. The story also tells of many traditions, always in the context of their place in the lives
of the Ojibway people. Readers, young and old, Indian or not, will learn, for example, of the custom of
the Ojibway to be guided throughout their lives by
dreams and of the importance of giving thanks and
honoring elders.

Ignatia Broker is uniquely qualified to tell this
story. An Ojibway elder and storyteller and an
enrolled member of White Earth Reservation, she
has experienced both reservation and urban life. She
is familiar with the old ways as well as the new. Ms.
Broker is one of those who organized, incorporated,
and built the Indian social groups in a time when In-

[4] J. W. Nunn, "Logging Around Ponsford," in Watrin, comp.,
The Ponsfordian, 18.

dian people had become aliens in the land of their birth, looking for a place to fit in. She was associated with the Upper Midwest American Indian Center, Minneapolis, the oldest organization of its kind in the Twin Cities, throughout its formative years. Ms. Broker has also endeavored to keep alive the traditions, beliefs, and history of the Ojibway; her attention to the elders, her research and writing, and her work with a variety of schools, agencies, and societies has greatly furthered this goal. Her other published work includes *Weegwahsimitig*, the story of the birch tree, and *Ahmik Nishgahdahzee*, a filmstrip and poster story of an angry beaver, both produced by the Indian Elementary Curriculum Project of the Minneapolis Public Schools. An Ojibway story that she tells is also included in *The Ojibwe: A History Resource Unit* produced by the Minnesota Historical Society.

In *Night Flying Woman* the narrator relates that there will be five generations of Ojibway who will make a circle. The first people will start the circle and the others will move from the Ojibway ways. The circle will be closed when the last generation again acts as the Ojibway did in years before: "There will be those who will ask questions and those who remember" before the circle closes. In this narrative, Ignatia Broker has honored us by searching her memory and remembering. All we have to do is listen.

New York City   *Paulette Fairbanks Molin*
May, 1983

PROLOGUE
The Forest Cries

"When the forest weeps, the
Anishinabe who listen will look
back at the years. In each generation of Ojibway there will be a person who will hear the si-si-gwa-d,
who will listen and remember and
pass it on to the children."

I GOT OFF the city bus and walked the short one-
and-a-half blocks home as I have been doing for
years around five o'clock each evening. Because this
evening was warm, I walked slower than usual, enjoying the look and feel of the early spring. The earth
that had been white was now brown, left uncov-
ered by the melting snow. This brown was turning
to green and the air was fragrant with the opening
of spring.

Daylight still lingered and as I walked I looked at
my neighborhood and thought about it. When I first
moved here in the mid-1950s this was a mixed neighborhood of Spanish-speaking people and Catholic

1

whites, and there were many children. Now the Spanish-speaking people are all gone. They left when the parochial school closed its doors, although the church is still here. Now the neighborhood is only four blocks long and two blocks wide, whittled down by urban renewal and the freeways which reach their tentacles all around us.

I reached my doorstep and sat enjoying the good day and remembering the past. It was funny, really, when I think about it. That day thirty years ago when we moved here, me and my children, we were the aliens looking for a place to fit in, looking for a chance of a new life, moving in among these people, some of whose 'forefathers' had displaced my ancestors for the same reason: looking for a new life. Their fathers were the aliens then, and now they, the children, are in possession of this land.

For a long time I was that Indian person with the two children. But it is good that children have a natural gift of accepting people, and so my children became a part of the neighborhood.

Thirty years in this neighborhood. My children went to school from here, they went to church from here, they were married from here and even though they are in faraway places they seem to have their roots here, for they had lived no other place while growing up.

I talked to my children, even when they were very small, about the ways of the Ojibway people. They were good children and they listened, but I had a feeling that they listened the same as when I read a story about the Bobbsey twins or Marco Polo. I was speaking of another people, removed from them by rock and roll, juvenile singers, and the bobbing movement of the new American dance.

My two, born and raised in Minneapolis, are of that generation of Ojibway who do not know what the reservation means, or the Bureau of Indian Affairs, or the tangled treaties and federal — so called — Indian laws which have spun their webs for a full century around the Native People, the First People of this land.

Now my children are urging me to recall all the stories and bits of information that I ever heard my grandparents or any of the older Ojibway tell. It is important, they say, because now their children are asking them. Others are saying the same thing. It is well that they are asking, for the Ojibway young must learn their cycle.

I have been abroad in this society, the dominating society, for two-thirds of my life, and yet I am a link in a chain to the past. Because of this, I shall do as they ask. I can close my eyes and I am back in the past.

I came to the Twin Cities from the reservation in 1941, the year Pearl Harbor was attacked. I went to work in a defense plant and took night classes in order to catch up on the schooling I had missed. I was twenty-two years old and aching for a permanent, settling-down kind of life, but the war years were unstable years for everyone, and more so for the Indian people.

Although employment was good because of the labor demand of the huge defense plants, Indian people faced discrimination in restaurants, night clubs, retail and department stores, in service organizations, public offices, and worst of all, in housing. I can remember hearing, "This room has been rented already, but I got a basement that has a room. I'll show you." I looked at the room. It had the usual rectangular window, and pipes ran overhead. The walls and floors were brown cement, but the man with a gift-giving tone in his voice said, "I'll put linoleum on the floor for you and you'll have a toilet all to yourself. You could wash at the laundry tubs."

There was of course, nothing listed with the War Price and Rationing Board, but the man said it would cost seven dollars a week. I know that he would have made the illegal offer only to an Indian because he knew of the desperate housing conditions we, the first Americans, faced.

I remember living in a room with six others. It was a housekeeping room, nine by twelve feet in size, and meant for one person. It was listed with the price agency at five dollars a week, but the good landlady collected five dollars from each of us each week. However, she did put in a bunk bed and a rollaway which I suppose was all right because we were on different shifts and slept different times anyway. It was cramped and crowded but we had a mutual respect. We sometimes shared our one room with others who had no place, so that there might be nine or ten of us. We could not let friends be out on the street without bed or board. As long as our landlady did not mind, we helped and gave a place of rest to other Ojibway people.

Our paydays were on different days and so whoever had money lent carfare and bought meat and vegetables. Stew was our daily fare because we had only a hot plate and one large kettle.

I mention this practice because I know other Indian people did the same thing, and sometimes whole families evolved from it. This was how we got a toehold in the urban areas – by helping each other. Perhaps this is the way nonmaterialistic people do. We were a sharing people and our tribal traits are still within us.

I think now that maybe it was a good thing, the migration of our people to the urban areas during the war years, because there, amongst the millions of people, we were brought to a brotherhood. We Indian people who worked in the war plants started a social group not only for the Ojibway but for the Dakota, the Arikara, the Menominee, the Gros Ventres, the Cree, the Oneida, and all those from other tribes and other states who had made the trek to something new. And because we, all, were isolated in this dominant society, we became an island from which a revival of spirit began.

It was not easy for any of us during the war years and it became more difficult after the war had ceased. Many Native People returned to the reservations after our soldiers came home from the foreign lands, but others like me stayed and took the buffeting and the difficulties shown us by an alien society.

The war plants closed and people were without jobs. The labor market tightened up and we, the Native People – even skilled workers – faced bias, prejudice, and active discrimination in employment.

I know because when I was released from my defense job I answered many advertisements and
always I was met with the words, "I'm sorry but we
don't hire Indians because they only last the two
weeks till payday. Then they quit."

It was around this time that I met and married a
veteran who was passing through to the reservation.
He got a job with the railroad. To be close to that job
and because of the bias in housing, we moved to the
capitol side of the river, to an area of St. Paul called
the river flats. It was a poor area. Many of the houses
had outdoor toilets; many were but tar-paper shacks.
Surprising, but it was so in this very large city. It was
here our two children were born and I, like a lot of
other Indian women, went out and did day work—
cleaning and scrubbing the homes of the middle-
income people.

Many Indian families lived on the river flats,
which became vibrant with their sharing. People
gave to each other because times were bad. No Indian family dared approach the relief and welfare
agencies of the Twin Cities. They knew that they
would only be given a bus ticket and be told to go
back to the reservation where the government would
take care of them as usual. This was the policy of the
public service agencies, and we put up with it by not
asking for the help to which we had a legal right. We
also suffered in other ways of their making. My husband was recalled to service and died in Korea. After
this I moved from the river flats. I took the clerical
training and got my first job at a health clinic.

Because my husband died fighting for a nation
designed for freedom for all, I felt that I must help

extend that freedom to our people. I joined a group of Indians who had banded together to form an Indian help agency. We built a welfare case to challenge the policy of sending our people back to the reservation, and we were successful. After that, the tide of Indians moving to Minnesota's urban areas increased, and today there are ten thousand of us. As the number grew, new-fangled types of Indian people came into being: those demanding what is in our treaties, those demanding service to our people, those working to provide these services—and all reaching back for identity.

When I see my people every day and know how they are doing, I do not feel so lost in the modern times. The children of our people who come to our agency have a questioning look, a dubious but seeking-to-learn look, and I truly believe that they are reaching back to learn those things of which they can be proud. Many of these children were born and raised in the urban areas and they do not make any distinctions as to their tribes. They do not say, "I am Ojibway," or "I am Dakota," or "I am Arapaho," but they say, "I am an Indian." Now they, too, are looking to their tribal identity.

These children are again honoring the Old People by asking them to speak, and I like other older people will search my memory and tell what I know. I, myself, shall tell you what I have heard my grandmother tell and I shall try to speak in the way she did and use the words that were hers.

My grandchildren,

I am glad that you, the young Ojibway of today, are seeking to learn the beliefs, the customs, and the practices of our people, for these things have too long been alive only within the memories of the Old Ones. I am glad that you are asking, for it has always been the custom for us to tell what must be passed on so that our ways will be known to the Ojibway children of the future.

Many times when I was a young girl I was fortunate to hear my grandmother tell of the lives and deeds of our grandfathers, grandmothers, and other people of our clan. I listened to these stories, but I really did not know their worth. "What good are these tales in today's world?" asked many people, never realizing that the Ojibway tales teach a philosophy for living. They tell of the purity of man and nature and keeping them in balance.

It is important that you learn the past and act accordingly, for that will assure us that we will always people the earth. I say this because our people who have gone before have said this. They have said that there will be five generations of Ojibway who will make a circle. The first people will start the circle and the others will move from the Ojibway ways. There will be those who will ask questions and those who remember, and the last generation will again act as the Ojibway have acted in years before. Then the circle will be closed.

I do not know which generation the children of today are, but the questions are beginning.

We, the Ojibway, are a forest people. A long time before a strange people came to this country, we lived east and north of this land now called Minnesota in the country of the eastern longhouses. Once we even lived on the big water of salt. We peopled both the north and south banks of what is now called the St. Lawrence River, and by 1770 we reached the north and south shores of what are now called the Great Lakes. We lived in harmony with our kinsmen of the Algonquin nation – the Ottawa, the Menominee, and the Potawatomi – for they, too, were forest peoples. We were the westernmost and perhaps the largest tribe of this nation. The forests were huge and thick, and they were filled with our brethren, the animal people.

We did not own the land acre by acre as is done today, but we respected the right of all people to share in the gifts given by the Great Being to the Anishinabe, which means us, the original people.

The Mi-de-wi-wi-n was a society within all Ojibway communities. Its basic philosophy was the prolonging of life and its practice was the use of herbs, the setting of bones, and the healing of wounds. The use of Mi-de-wi-wi-n rites was restricted to the society's members. They were consulted for their deeper knowledge of medicine.

The gathering and use of herbs was not, however, restricted to the Mi-de-wi-wi-n. Most adult Ojibway had a general knowledge of herbs and medicine, and there were also the Medicine People who had a greater knowledge. This they taught to the younger members of the family so that the practice continued from one generation to the next.

Our family traveled a tortuous path, trying to escape alien contact and retain a satisfying life. As the strange new people, the voyageurs, came into our homeland, pushing and disrupting, many of the Ojibway met with them and became their friends. But our family group preferred to remain in the paths of our ancestors. They moved toward the setting sun and southward to the land of lakes and rivers. They would not deal with the strange people. We, the descendants who now live in the urban areas or on the reservation, have never put a foot in the many places where our ancestors lived, but our roots are in the land of forests where they made their homes.

The best way to learn why we were separated from the first generation is to tell you about the people who lived then. This I shall do by telling you of my great-great-grandmother, who is your grandmother five times removed. Her name was Ni-bo-wi-se-gwe, which means Night Flying Woman. Her nickname was Oona.

The village in which Oona was born was very large and had many lodges. It was north and west of the Lake of Nettles, which is now called Nett Lake, where the A-sa-bi-ig-go-na-ya, the People of the Nettle Fibers, lived. Although Ojibway people had been there many years, they were still thought of as newcomers by the People of the Nettle Fibers. But indeed they had been together a long, long time. They had shared the joy of birth and the sadness of the last journey. They had feasted together in time of plenty and had shared in time of little. They had been happy and there had always been peace among them.

In the early 1800s the strangers, those people who had robbed the white pine from the land of the

Cherokee, began looking at the tall trees in the forests of the Ojibway. Soon their clamor reached the communities of the Ojibway. "We need lumber for building homes and ships and the shops in our towns." The industry that ate the forests became king and then the Great White Father, who was declared chief of all the people, sent treaty papers to the Ojibway. Six times groups of Ojibway were required to mark the treaties. Each time their lands passed into the hands of the alien peoples, and each group was required to move to a Native Area. These Native Areas are now called the Chippewa reservations of Minnesota.

The strangers rapidly settled in the Ojibway territory. They soon surrounded the Native Areas and ripped away the forests. After them came more strangers who plowed the lands and made the laws and demanded the restriction of the Ojibway to the Native Areas. The council fires burned low because the agents of the strangers now said what must be so and what the Ojibway must do. Then came the peoples with the books, each saying his was the best. They told the Ojibway to mend their ways and follow the words of the book.

This is the time when Oona lived and these were the things that Oona faced. The adjustments that Oona and her family group made were much the same as those made by other family groups. This was the time when the generations of Ojibway began the travel on the circle away from the beginning, clinging in memory to what had been before. What was before must again be there when the circle closes.

Ni-bo-wi-se-gwe

NI-BO-WI-SE-GWE is a great-great-grandmother to many people of the Wolf and Fish clans, and in our family we speak of her with pride. She was a great and unusual woman, and there are many stories told of her life and ways.

As it is told, many of the events and circumstances pertaining to Ni-bo-wi-se-gwe were unusual, even from the time before her birth. Her father, Me-ow-ga-bo (Outstanding), and mother, Wa-wi-e-cu-mig-go-gwe (Round Earth), were young, healthy, and strong. Usually such Ojibway couples have children early in marriage, and often they have at least five. But it was not so with this young couple. They had been three years together, a long time, and they had not had a child. The people of their village began to wonder and feel a sadness for the young couple. After the third year, Ni-bo-wi-se-gwe was born, and she was the only child.

The time of her birth was after the blueberry gathering and before the wild-rice harvesting. The day began bright and sunny, and it was so when Wa-wi-e-cu-mig-go-gwe felt the first pangs of birth. Just before the sun was high in the sky, at the exact time of birth, the sun and moon crossed paths and there was a pitch darkness. In this darkness the first wail of the child was heard, and because of this her parents knew that the tiny girl would be different. But they felt it was good because she was born of love and joy.

So out of the darkness, called the eclipse, was born a person who became strong and gave strength, who became wise and lent this wisdom to her people, who became part of the generation of chaos and change.

Me-ow-ga-bo and Wa-wi-e-cu-mig-go-gwe were happy, for it was a time of plenty. The velvet of the forest shone as soft and bright as the love they had for Tiny Girl. They had waited a long time for their child. Now that they were fulfilled, they would fill the life of their child with all that was necessary to honor her and thus the people and the Gitchi Mani-to, the Great Spirit.

Three weeks after birth, according to the custom of the people, came the time when the naming must be planned. The spirit of every person must be honored with a name, a song, and an animal. Tiny Girl must be given a name, and she must be given in honor to her grandparents.

Me-ow-ga-bo and Wa-wi-e-cu-mig-go-gwe consulted with Grandfather and Grandmother and decided that A-wa-sa-si (Bullhead) should be the namer, for A-wa-sa-si was old and wise and good. A-wa-sa-si was the storyteller, and when she placed her hands on the heads of the children, their crying and fears were stilled. The family lit a pipe and offered it to the Gitchi Manito. Then they sent Tiny

Girl's cap with a bag of kin-nik-a-nik inside to old
A-wa-sa-si. If A-wa-sa-si accepted the cap and
smoked the kin-nik-a-nik it meant that she would,
indeed, be the namer.

A-wa-sa-si took the cap and smiled, for it pleased
her to be the namer. First she went into the forest to
choose the medicine for the animal bag that she
would make and give to the baby. Then she visited
the child and returned to the forest to meditate and
to choose an animal and a song. She visited Tiny Girl
again. A day was set for the naming feast, and the
family sent kin-nik-a-nik to all the people in the
village to let them know that they were to come.

The family began to prepare the feast for the
naming ceremony. There would be much food, for it
was after the ricing time when food was stored and
buried. Acorns were roasted. Hazel nuts were
ground and mixed with dried berries to make small
cakes. Ma-no-min, the precious wild rice, was
popped and mixed with si-s-sa-ba-gwa-d, the maple
sugar. There would be fish, deer, and rabbit for all,
but the heads of the bear and buffalo were reserved
for the Old Ones of the Mi-de-wi-wi-n.

The ceremony and feast were held in the
beautiful autumn season. Although the days were
cooling, they were yet sunny. The green of the forest
was turning to orange, gold, and brown; this orange,
gold, and brown fell and cushioned the earth and reflected the glory of the trees.

All the people of the village arrived bringing gifts.
They came to hear the honor of the name given to
the child of Me-ow-ga-bo and Wa-wi-e-cu-mig-go-
gwe, for by honoring a child the people also honored

the Gitchi Manito. A-wa-sa-si had chosen the name Ni-bo-wi-se-gwe, which means Night Flying Woman, because Tiny Girl had been born during the darkness of the day. A-wa-sa-si said that the shadows when the sun left the earth and the shadows when the day began would be the best time for her. But because Ni-bo-wi-se-gwe was such a long name for tiny tongues, the child was soon called Oona, for her first laughing sound.

Oona's first months were like those of all Ojibway children. The Ojibway know that a learning process begins at birth and that a baby's first learning experience is watching. So, as soon as possible, Oona was laced into a cradleboard and placed where she could see her family at work and at play. She watched Grandmother lacing muk-kuk-ko-ons-sug, the strong birch-bark containers, or winding wi-go-b, the tough string made from the bark of trees. People talked to her about things they saw and did. Oona was happy. She would look into the shadows in the lodge and smile, and the people would remember the time she came.

Being strapped in the cradleboard was also the beginning of her experience in restraint. She began to learn this in the customary way. At certain times when she cried, a brushy stick was scraped across her face and her lips were pinched. These actions would be repeated if the family needed to make a silent journey; then Oona would know she must not cry. It was a matter of survival, especially if there were enemies in the forest.

During the first year of Oona's life the winter white piled high around the lodges, but she did not know this for inside the lodge all was warm and snug. The fire in the middle of the lodge leaped and shone and made patterns that made Oona laugh and coo. Many times old A-wa-sa-si would be in the lodge with Grandmother, for these two watched over Oona. Mother would go about her work, and often she would stop and whisper softly to Oona. Sometimes she made tiny clothes when she sat watching the meat roast over the fire. Father would come in blowing cold air and smiling, his strength and presence making everyone feel that all was well.

When the winter white turned to water, Oona, still in the cradle, went to the maple-sugar bush with the family. In the summer Oona tasted berries fresh from the bush. She walked her first steps in the fall at ricing time. For five years Oona's cycle of life was the same. Summer camp to ricing camp to winter village to sugar bush to planting time to summer camp. These years were filled with love and laughter and this cycle was the cycle of life of our people, the Ojibway.

It was the beautiful spring season. The days now were warm and clear and the sun shone through the new green of the trees. The stately birch, which had looked ghostly all through the winter, was sprinkled with the green. Once again it offered its yearly gift of bark to the forest people. Pale flowers, the violet and the crocus, lifted their faces and lent their fragile scent to the forest air, blending with the village smell of the wood fires and burning cedar leaves. The waters in the brooks whispered back and forth with the trees. Squirrels came out from their winter homes and they too chattered back and forth, holding their tails up high. This was a sign foretelling warmth for the coming days. Other Forest Brothers were standing, lean but shining, ready for another cycle of birth and life. Everything was so new, fresh, and good.

There was much excitement in the Ojibway village and the children felt it. It made them fearful. A do-daim, or clansman, from the east was visiting and the people held a feast in his honor. After the feast, in the evening, the people met in council to hear the news of the do-daim. He told of a strange people whose skins were as pale as the winter white and whose eyes were blue or green or gray.

"Yes," said A-bo-wi-ghi-shi-g (Warm Sky), the village leader, "I have seen these strangers."

"I also," said others.

"These strangers," said the do-daim, "are again asking the Ojibway to mark a paper. All the leaders of the A-sa-bi-ig-go-na-ya, the Nettle Fiber People, are to do this. The Ojibway to the east have made the mark, and now they are on the big water where they must stay forever. The strangers promised never to enter their forests but they came anyway to trade for the coats of the Animal Brothers. I have a muk-kuk they gave me, and I will leave it to you. It sits right on the fire and does not crack. It is called iron kettle, and the strangers have promised many of these when the papers are marked."

"Have you studied these strangers well? Are they good people, or are they those who will be enemies?" asked A-bo-wi-ghi-shi-g.

"Some are kind. Others speak good. Others smile

when they think they are deceiving," replied the do-daim. "Many of the Ojibway have stayed with these people, but soon our people had great coughs and there were bumps on their skins, and they were given water that made them forget."

"I have seen these strangers before. They have come into the forests many times," said Grandfather. "I know that they desire the furs of our animal friends and wish to give us the strange things."

"Yes," said the do-daim, "these strangers are asking the Ojibway to trap the Animal Brothers. They give a stick that roars and that can kill faster than an arrow."

"Also," said Grandfather, "I have seen the men with the long dress. They speak many words about Gitchi Manito, the Great Spirit. And I have seen the men with the fire sticks. They have followed the Chi-si-bi (Mississippi) to its source."

"But now," said the do-daim, "these strangers are many. They intend to stay, for they are building lodges and planting food. Far to the east, the forests of the Eastern Keepers have been ripped from the face of the earth and the doors of the longhouses have been sealed.

"These strangers fight among themselves. They fought and killed each other for the land of the Mo-wi-ga-n (Mohegan) and now again they are fighting in the land of the Che-ro-ki (Cherokee).

"Our kinsmen, the O-ma-no-ma-ni-g (Menomi-nee), the Wild Rice People, are crowded at the edge of the big water, and the O-da-wa (Ottawa) have crossed the big water. The O-bo-da-wa-da-mi-g (Potawatomi) have gone south, many of them. The Mi-s-gwa-ghi (Fox) are shivering with cold and hunger now. They are but a handful in number.

"Down by the Chi-si-bi at the place where the small gulls fly, the forests have become smaller. Strangers are there in great number. All day long they cut the trees and send them down the river. Although these strangers have said they will stay to the rising sun, already they are looking this way, for soon there will be no forest where they are now.

"Yes, my brothers," said the do-daim, "these strangers are looking this way."

When the do-daim left, the council fires burned. The people discussed what he had said.

A-bo-wi-ghi-shi-g, the leader, said, "We cannot escape for long the meeting with these strange people. Our kinsmen on the Chi-o-ni-ga-mig (Lake Superior) have marked the paper and now they must forever stay at O-bi-mi-wi-i-to-n (Grand Portage), the carrying place. Also, I have been to where the Chi-si-bi and the A-bwa-na-g (Minnesota) waters meet. I have seen the strangers' lodges there. The lodges are many and the men called soldiers are many. They will forever be there, for they plant the corn."

Oona's grandfather said, "I also have been to the land where the small gulls live, where the strangers push the forest poles into the big river. I have seen their lodges and their planting. Soon all will be planted. But I have also been to the rainy country. The men who desire the furs are few there now. They use the waters only to pass on to the big north country, and this is seldom. The forests are thick there, and beneath the trees the earth is soft and boggy so the planting would not be good, although there are many dry places deep within the bogs. I am thinking that I shall take my family there and maybe escape these strangers for a while."

"Yes," said A-bo-wi-ghi-shi-g, "we shall do that. Those who wish to go with you will lay a stick in a pile. I shall take the others to the strangers at the Lake of Nettles if this must be so. But we all must move soon in order to plant the seed in our new places and find the ricing beds and the sugar bush."

The people met and talked for three days on the hill outside the village. They spoke of the many good things that had always been. Of grandfathers and grandmothers who were the dust of the forests. Of those who would be left in the journeying places. The women listened and there was a wailing sound to their voices when they talked together.

On the eve of the third day, the men smoked the pipe of peace in council and passed around the sacred kin-nik-a-nik. The voices of the people became stilled and a quiet purpose was reflected in their faces. The whole forest became silent.

Little Oona awoke one bright new day to the busy stirrings of the village. She had felt the excitement of the past few days, and she was fearful. "Bis-in-d-an, listen," Oona whispered to herself, heeding one of her first lessons. "Listen, and you will hear the patterns of life. Are they the same, or is there a change in the sounds?" So Oona listened. "Something different is happening today," Oona whispered again to herself. Quickly she rolled out from under the rabbitskin robe, dressed, and went out of the lodge. She saw Grandfather and Grandmother making bundles of food and clothing.

Oona was only five years old but she was already trained in many of the ways of a good Ojibway. She knew almost all that she could not do and all that she must learn to do. She went to her grandparents and stood before them with eyes cast down, knowing she could not speak the many questions she wished to ask, for they who are wise must speak first. Always, the first words spoken should be from the older people.

Oona wanted to look up at her grandfather's face, a face that was lined with many years. She had always sought comfort from her grandfather, who had a special look just for her. He would smile with his eyes and she felt well and cared for.

"Oona, my child," said Grandfather, "I hope you have slept well. I know by the roundness of your eyes that you are wondering what is doing today." Grandfather paused, sat down, and stretched out his hand to Oona. "Take my hand, and I will tell you what your eyes ask.

"Remember this day, my child," Grandfather continued. "For all of your small life, this village, this place, has been your home, but now we must move toward the setting sun. We have been happy here and we have lived here a long, long time. A very long time even before you were born. At the council it was decided that we shall seek a new place. We move because there is another people who are fast coming into the forest lands. Their ways are different and we wish to be free of them for as long as we can.

"Take the things you wish to take – your corn doll and rubbing rock toy. Put them in a bundle. There is room." Grandfather smiled and Oona felt comforted. She accepted the thoughts of change. With a feeling of excitement and anticipation, she went and stood before her mother.

"Mother," said Oona, "who will be leaving with us?"

"There will be eight families," replied Mother. "Four of your uncles and their families and three families of the do-daim of the Muk-kwa, and of course old A-wa-sa-si. Grandfather, since he is the oldest, will be the leader."

"When shall we be leaving, Mother?"

"We shall leave in a while, for we are all packed and the men have gone to get the canoes from the place of hiding. We must leave before the others go to the Lake of Nettles to be counted. That way the strange people will not know that we are not doing what they demand."

Mother looked down at her fragile daughter, she who was much smaller than the other children of her age. She brushed Oona's black shining hair and lifted up the small oval face with the huge dark eyes.

"It is sad to be leaving, my Oona," said Mother, "but in one's life there are many times when one must leave a place of happiness for the unknown. I have done this many times, but the beauty of a life remains forever in the heart. You must remember the beauty that was here. Go, my daughter, and say the words of friendship to those who were your playmates."

Oona made up her little bundle. Then she went to find her cousin, E-quay (Lady). They joined hands and circled the camp, smiling the smile of friendship to those they would not see again. They then went to the river to wait for the men and the canoes.

Six Days' Journey

THEY WOULD TRAVEL a tortuous way, winding back and forth, leaving no path to follow. It would be a silent, secret journey so that the strangers in the forest would not know that people were fleeing. The children were told of the silence they must keep, and the babies' mouths were pinched so that they, too, understood that they must not make a crying sound.

When the men brought the canoes, the silent people placed their bundles inside. They took only their stores of maple sugar and rice, si-s-sa-ba-gwa-d and ma-no-min, corn, dried meat, and berries. Their only clothing was what they would need on the journey.

The other people of the village did not come to see them off, so that they would look like the usual small group going on a short trip. Grandfather's canoe was first in line. He had with him Grandmother and four small grandchildren. Oona rode with Father and Mother and A-wa-sa-si. The older children paddled their own canoes, and they were responsible for keeping the dogs quiet.

This first river was almost straight. It was quiet and shallow. The boys called it Ni-gi, my friend, and the girls called it Ni-shi-ma, my younger kin. It would take two days on this river before they would reach the next stage of their journey.

Oona sat in the canoe between A-wa-sa-si and Father. She liked riding in the canoe. The motion reminded her of being in a cradle. This was only her second canoe trip, and she liked being on the river. She looked at the trees that were thick along the river banks, at the oaks with their branches reaching to the sky, at the birch and the popple gleaming white in the sun. The rapid change of the forest made Oona feel that the trees were moving instead of the canoe. Oona whispered to herself, "Poor Trees, we are leaving, but you will be gone too after the strangers come." She saw the squirrels scamper back and forth, their tails waving proudly. She thought, "Poor squirrels, where will you go after the strangers come?" She thought of the deer and the beaver and she whispered, "Poor Brothers, where will you go when the strangers come?"

"Mother," said Oona, "shall we ever come back?"

"I think not, my daughter. We shall find a new place. We shall be happy and the old place will always be ours, for the bones of our uncles, our aunts, our grandmothers, and our grandfathers have blended with the earth there and the strangers cannot erase that."

Oona watched her mother swing the paddle from side to side. She was a small woman but she was strong. Oona thought, "My mother's face is different from the other women's in the village. Their faces are round, but my mother's is square. She is different. I don't know why. My mother does not speak as much as the other women but she listens and she smiles."

Then Oona thought of her father, who was sitting in the rear of the canoe. Every once in a while he would lean forward and just to tease her, he would blow on her neck. She thought, "My father is a laughing person. He is always playing tricks on me. He is the strongest and the bravest and the best hunter in the forest. I shall be like both my father and my mother."

As the sun rose high in the sky, it sent its rays to warm the people. Oona felt this warmth on her back and she grew sleepy. She said to herself, "I must keep my eyes open. I want to see everything," but the sunlight and the lapping of the water soon lulled her to sleep. When she awoke her father was lifting her from the canoe onto a wooded bank. He saw that she was awake and he said, "Ha, little sly one, only little owls sleep during the day, but maybe you are a little owl for your eyes are bigger than your face."

"Is this the new place, Father?" asked Oona.

"No, my daughter," replied Father. "We shall stay here only through the night. We must rest for we have a long, long journey yet."

After all the families had gathered in a forest glade near the river and after the men had hidden the canoes, Grandfather sprinkled kin-nik-a-nik and said, "We have had a good day and by this we give thanks."

They set up no lodges because this was only a temporary place, but they lit campfires and soon the women were busy preparing the evening meal. Precious ma-no-min and hot water were mixed together in muk-kuk-ko-ons-sug and placed high over the fires. Along with dried meat and dried berries there were fresh fish, for this was the time fish also travel the rivers to the summer places.

After the meal the children were wrapped in robes and placed near the warming fires. Because the campfires would burn all night, the men would take turns circling the camp, watching for strangers. Before the night grew long there was talking, laughing, and joking. No one mentioned the old place.

The second day's journey was much like the first. It seemed longer to Oona, and she grew tired of being in the canoe. The third day there was a change. The people walked. The women and children carried the bundles and the men went ahead carrying the canoes.

Oona carried her little bundle like the rest. She walked and walked and she thought, "I have walked forever." But finally camp was made for the third night. This one was more enjoyable. The children had time to play, to explore the woods, and to see the Animal Brothers.

The next day they walked again with the bundles and canoes, but before the sun had left the sky they came to another river and made camp. Oona, who was very tired of walking, was happy that they would again be traveling by canoe.

A short journey on this river brought them to a lake. They crossed the lake, then followed the shoreline to the west until they reached another river. This third river was different from the others. First it was as wide as a long lake, then very narrow. All along the shore, in the water, lay fallen trees and broken stumps. Oona heard her father say, "The river is shallow. There must be many fish hiding under the fallen trees, and that would make this a land of Muk-kwa, the bear. It is a good sign, for many of our people are of the Muk-kwa do-daim."

The journey through the river of fallen trees took them to another lake, small and beautiful, with high stone at its edges. On top of the stone, trees towered to the sky, hiding the sun. It seemed to Oona that they were in a land of shadows, even though sunlight danced on the water as it escaped through the trees. The people circled this lake almost completely looking for an opening. They passed through into another small lake, and although the sun was not quite set, they decided to camp there.

When everyone was ashore the children waited patiently, although they were eager to explore. They waited for Grandfather to choose the campsite and sprinkle out the precious kin-nik-a-nik. Then the people lit campfires and the women put venison on to roast along with the ma-no-min. Everyone helped build temporary shelters of brush and small poles, after which the children went swimming and wading. It was a good camp, and a feeling of strength and comfort was renewed.

On this, the fifth night of their travels, after the people had given thanks and eaten the evening meal, there was a firelight council. The people decided to stay on this small lake for two days while three of the men went deep into the forest to look for the new place.

The next morning, very early, Grandfather, Oldest Uncle, and Father walked into the thick forest.

Oona did not see them leave, for she was sleeping soundly. When Mother told her that they were gone, Oona looked at the forest fearfully. It seemed very unfriendly. She thought, "It has swallowed up my grandfather and father." She became fretful.

Mother said, "Daughter, look at the forest again but do not look and see only the dark and shadows. Instead, look at the trees, each one, as many as you can. Then tell me what you think."

Oona looked at the trees. Then she walked to the forest's edge to see them better. There were many, many kinds of trees. Some were tall, so tall that they must surely touch the sky, thought Oona. Instead of leaves they had needles that were long and pointed like porcupine quills. Beneath these tall trees smaller ones reached up, as if in friendship. As Oona looked at the trees, she heard the si-si-gwa-d — the murmuring that the trees do when they brush their branches together. It was a friendly sound, and the sun sent sparkles through the si-si-gwa-d that chased the shadows. Suddenly the forest seemed different to Oona, and she knew that Grandfather, Oldest Uncle, and Father had gone into a friendly place.

"Mother," said Oona, "I have the feeling now that the trees are glad we are here. The forest is happy and I know that we will be happy, too."

"That is good, my daughter, for I also have the feeling that this will be a good and happy place." A-wa-sa-si and Grandmother, who had been listening, nodded their heads in agreement.

A-wa-sa-si said, "The forests have never failed the Ojibway. The trees are the glory of the Gitchi Manito. The trees, for as long as they shall stand, will give shelter and life to the Anishinabe and the Animal Brothers. They are a gift. As long as the Ojibway are beneath, the trees will murmur with contentment. When the Ojibway and the Animal Brothers are gone, the forest will weep and this will be reflected in the sound of the si-si-gwa-d. My grandmother told me this is so, and her grandmother told her. When the forest weeps, the Anishinabe who listen will look back at the years. In each generation of Ojibway there will be a person who will hear the si-si-gwa-d, who will listen and remember and pass it on to the children. Remembering our past and acting accordingly will ensure that we, the Ojibway, will always people the earth. The trees have patience and so they have stood and have seen many generations of Ojibway. Yet will there be more, and yet will they see more."

Oona stood looking at the forest, and she repeated, silently, the words she had just heard. She smiled within because she was pleased to have been given an important message.

"Mother," said Oona, "I know that I have been honored by being told these words. I shall repeat them many times and I shall be patient as I wait for Grandfather, Oldest Uncle, and Father."

Mother was also pleased and she, too, smiled within, for she knew that A-wa-sa-si meant to speak other important words to Oona. "Yes," she said, "we are both honored. But now we must prepare for the last part of the journey."

Oona and Mother went to the river to get a lightweight sapling to make a bi-mi-wi-t-gi-ga-n, a travois, to use on the last lap of the journey. They

cut two poles and a bar from the sapling. They attached a stretched skin to the poles, lacing it with wi-
go-b. The bar was used to separate the poles and
keep the skin stretched. They would use the travois
as a carryall.

When Mother indicated that the work was done,
Oona went swimming and wading with the other
small girls. Then they trailed down the river to watch
the beaver build his home. They respected Brother
Beaver. They knew he had special powers and could
cut down a tree and make a new path for a river.
They saw the deer, fat and heavy with their unborn
young. They saw the foxes traveling to the south-
lands to seek the prairie chickens and the pheasants.
They saw the geese flying overhead and heard them
honking from a distant marsh or shallow water.
They saw the little tadpoles swimming in the still,
cold water.

That evening as Mother and Oona waited for
sleep to come, Oona said, "Mother, the whole forest
has the sound of new life. Is it a good sign that we
are building a new life, too?"

"Yes, it is a good sign," said Mother.

On the second day, when the sun was lowering
itself in the west, Grandfather, Oldest Uncle, and
Father returned. Kin-nik-a-nik was passed from
hand to hand and a feast of fish eyes and fish eggs
was served to the three seekers. At the gathering
around the campfires Grandfather spoke.

"Indeed," he said, "we are favored, for just a
day's walk to the east there is a place. It is thick with
trees, and among the rocks, high to the side, is a
water that springs from the earth. This will be the

place if it is so agreed. One must walk through many soft and dangerous marshes to get there. For this reason it may not be seen by the strangers for a long time."

Again the kin-nik-a-nik was passed around. The people agreed that the new place had been found. That night peace and contentment hovered over the sleeping people as well as the rest of the forest.

In the morning, very early, the people made ready to start out, for they were anxious to reach the new home. After the morning meal they hid the canoes and took down the lodges. They scattered the brush and hid the poles. They buried the ashes of the campfires and spread pine needles over them so it would look as if they had never been there. When all was done, they walked into the forest.

As she walked, Oona felt that she was entering a new land. The pine forest was dark, much darker than on the river, but it was a sheltering darkness. Small patches of sunlight hit the ground and made many little sparkles that sometimes danced over Oona's face. The branches of the trees were high, so high that Oona had to lean far back in order to look at them. Beneath her feet the earth was cushioned with thousands and thousands of rust-colored needles. They gave the forest a reddish glow. It was pleasant and cool and the si-si-gwa-d murmured a peaceful sound of welcome.

"This is nice," said Oona to Mother. "I could walk on this forever. It is like standing on A-wa-sa-si's bearskin rug."

"Save your energy," replied Mother. "There is much ahead."

As they went deeper into the forest the earth beneath them became wet and boggy. Green moss and pine needles covered the boggy places and hid them so that the people stepped into holes. It was hard to find firm places to walk, and Mother was having great difficulty pulling the travois. Finally, when the travois anchored in a deep hole, she abandoned it. She and Oona made up bundles to carry and hid others to be fetched later.

Old A-wa-sa-si began to tire. Mother and Oona divided A-wa-sa-si's bundle, took what was needed, and hid everything else. They stopped often and sat on fallen trees to let her rest. They began to fall far behind, although they sometimes came upon others who were also resting. Those ahead left a trail.

When the earth became firm again and the trees fewer, the trail began to wind upward. There were boulders to walk around, and there were rocks: big rocks, small rocks, white rocks, and black rocks. Growing around them were ferns and little blueberry bushes. Mother and A-wa-sa-si sat on the large rocks and Oona climbed the boulders. From there, she could see the tops of the trees in the forest below.

When the sun began to travel downward the people too began to climb down from the high, rocky place. The trees again were popple, birch, and evergreen. When the sun said goodbye and the shadows deepened among the trees and bushes, the people quickened their paces for they could smell the smoke of wood fires. Father, who had led the way and prepared the campfires, came to meet them. He took their bundles and hurried back to help A-wa-sa-si. Mother and Oona walked as quickly as they could. Soon Oona and A-wa-sa-si were warming their toes at the fire. Oona looked and saw Grandfather and Grandmother. She smiled as she saw the faces of the people. She whispered to herself, "We are all here. This is the new place." She was content and fell asleep. So tired were the people that they slept as soon as they reached the fires, without eating the precious ma-no-min.

The Rainy Country

THE NEW PLACE WAS in a sheltered grove with towering pines all around. The first few days were busy ones. The people chose the spot for building and decided where each lodge would stand. Then they sprinkled an offering of kin-nik-a-nik. Since these new homes would be permanent, the people used care in planning and building them.

The women cut and stripped the bark from the basswood trees. Then they split this inner bark and spruce roots into strips to make wi-go-b. They soaked the strips in the river until they were quite strong, then spliced and wound the material into balls.

The men cut and peeled saplings for lodge poles. Some they bent into half-moons, tying the ends together. These too were put in water. After drying they stayed in the shape of a curve. When the poles were ready, the straight ones were anchored in the earth to form a circle and the bent ones were tied to the straight poles to make a dome. Others were put around the dome horizontally and fastened to the lodge poles with the wi-go-b. When this process was complete, the lodge frames were up.

The women wove reed mats and cut birch bark. They fastened the mats around the base of the lodge frames and put overlapping birch-bark sheets on the upper part. Then the lodges were ready.

The children cut the brush to make a clearing and the older ones set up fire racks. They hauled rocks and stones for the pits and made hammocks for the babies.

Father, Mother, and Oona built A-wa-sa-si's lodge and helped her prepare her home. They retrieved their bundles from the walking journey. They were prepared for the new life.

The lodges were grouped around an open space like a horseshoe, and all of them faced the rising sun. Grandfather's lodge was farthest east, because he was the leader. A-wa-sa-si's stood alone, behind and north of the others, for this was her wish. Beyond the new place was a steep hill where the water came from the earth. It rolled down to the meadow below and then off to the small lake.

"Mother," said Oona, "our lodge looks huge and strong. Will we be building a summer lodge elsewhere, or a blueberry lodge?"

"No," replied Mother. "Our lives must now revolve around this lodge, because we must not meet the strangers. But remember that we, the Ojibway, have always moved freely from a summer place to a winter place, with a blueberry place, a ricing place, and a sugar bush in between. It was decided that only sugar lodges will be built, if a good sugar bush is found. When we camp elsewhere for ricing or picking berries, we must destroy all traces of our stay and we must erase our trails."

When the village was built and a routine established, the people held a feast and ceremony. It was a good feast, mostly of fish, for the Animal Brothers were carrying their young. There were games and races, songs and dances. In the evening at the ceremony the Ojibway offered thanks to the Gitchi Manito. He had favored them with good weather all through the journey and had kept them all well to arrive safely. He had given them a good new place and welcomed them with a gift of plenty. The kin-nik-a-nik was passed around and smoked by the older people. Thus they offered thanks to the Great Spirit. The people would respect His gifts.

The full, spring-scented breath of Grandmother Earth was blowing everywhere. The flowers opened into pastel colors and the children heard the lilting of the Sky Brothers calling to them, "Come and see." As soon as they finished their duties to the elders, they heeded the call, following the trickle of water over the rocks and down to a small, clear, green-water lake. They walked through the forest to the other side of the little lake and came to a swampy meadow where cattails and yellow flowers waved in the sun. They smelled the sweetness of the meadow and saw the gift of the red kin-nik-a-nik all around.

They had to explore, for they needed to know the land in which they lived. They needed to listen to the everyday sounds and remember them. The girls as well as the boys had to learn the rocks and meadows and make trails that only they would see and know. Then, if ever the village were attacked, the children could run to their forest hiding places.

Oona and the other five- and six-year-olds stayed together, for they were the youngest explorers. They hid in the tall meadow grass or lay beneath a tree to watch the passing clouds. They knew when they saw a misty fog hovering over the lowlands that the red root and the sour green gooseberries would be waiting there at harvest time. They passed the doorways of the Animal Brothers, those who lived in the bramble bush and those who dug within the earth. They knew that the brothers watched them passing by. They looked for the sweet grass, the berry vines, and the peppermint plant. They would remember what they saw and heard, for they must tell all of this to A-wa-sa-si, their grandmothers, and mothers.

After the sun began its lowering, they walked back to their homes, for this was the time of work for them. It was time for the evening meal and for watching the little ones.

"Mother," said Oona, "I like this new place. The trees are so tall and so thick, and there are boglands all around, always with a mist over them. The treetops become lost in the mist, and yet there are little trees bending over the water and the whole earth smells like the sweetness of the grass."

"Yes, my daughter," said Mother. "This is a good place. We will be happy here."

Every morning in the early hours, Oona went to the lodge of Grandfather and Grandmother. It was a welcoming lodge, warm and cozy with the smell of cedar and pine. Oona felt good there. She sat before her grandparents with eyes cast down, watching them do the many tasks of life and listening as they spoke of the animal ways.

Grandmother often sewed robes of fur. Her hands were very fast as she made the holes in the skins. She used a mi-go-s, a tool made of a sharp bone stuck into a wooden bar. Oona, as she sat watching, often thought, "Will my hands be as fast as hers?" Grandfather was a good trapper so there were many furs and many quills of the porcupine. Mother dyed these quills and made beautiful patterns on deerskin. She was of the north and knew how it was done.

Oona soon learned to cut deer hide with a sharp beaver's tooth and to thread kernels of corn for a necklace. Many times Oona went with Grandmother and A-wa-sa-si into the forest to gather the plants for healing and the plants for coloring the porcupine quills and the feathers. She learned to pick on-da-g-o-ba-go-sin, the peppermint plant, wi-ni-shi-ba-go-sin, the evergreen bush, and ma-s-gi-go-ba-go-n, the swamp leaves. Other times Oona went with Grandfather to the swampy meadow to cut the red willow for the kin-nik-a-nik. She saw Grandfather pull a beaver from the water. Grandfather showed Oona how to place a fish trap and loop a noose for wa-bo-os, the rabbit.

Every evening, after a day of playing, exploring, and learning, Oona returned to the lodge of Grandfather and Grandmother. She sat before them, and they said, "Our daughter, what has been done today? Can you ask in truth and peace, 'Have I done enough today to earn the right to live tomorrow?' "

Oona would count and think about the things she had done that day. Grandmother would touch her fingers to the back of Oona's hand, and Grandfather would place his hand on her head in blessing.

Almost daily Oona went to the lodge of her cousin E-quay, who was her age. E-quay's mother, On-da-g (Crow), was Father's sister. Her family counted six children. One brother was older than E-quay and three were younger, and another brother had just been born in the new place. Oona liked to go to the home of E-quay because of New Brother. Each time she visited she wished for a brother of her own. E-quay knew how Oona felt and one day she said, "Would you like to hold New Brother?" Oona picked up New Brother and sat with him in her lap. His skin was soft and brown, his hair was long and felt like cornsilk. His eyes were big and black. He smiled sweetly at Oona and wrapped his fingers around her thumb. Second small brother, who was called A-na-gwa-d (Cloud), snuggled up to Oona and poked New Brother in the stomach. Everybody laughed, for they all knew that A-na-gwa-d still wished to be the baby. When New Brother got sleepy, Oona was allowed to wrap him in the cradle-board.

When all was quiet in the lodge, Oona went to stand before Aunt On-da-g with eyes cast down.

"What is it, my child?" asked Aunt On-da-g.

"Shall I help you plant?" said Oona.

"Yes, my child, you shall help me plant and you shall help me gather in the wild food. After two darknesses we shall do the planting." Aunt On-da-g had been the best gardener at the old place and she would now be the one responsible for planting and for gathering the wild vegetables. She was always glad to show the art of gardening and harvesting to the young people.

When Oona and E-quay left this happy lodge, they walked around to the back and into a little thicket. There E-quay's father worked in a small shelter. When he saw Oona, he called "Nuco" just to tease her. This was the way all uncles teased their nieces. Uncle, whose name was Ge-pa-gwa-na-gwa-d, which means Thick Cloud, was a very small man. He did not hunt or fish. Instead he was a maker of bows and arrows, fish traps, snowshoes, pipes, and drums. He supplied others with these tools. He was often given the best of the game and fish, for his bows and arrows were very highly prized. Uncle Ge-pa-gwa-na-gwa-d sat in the far back of the small shelter. Before him was a hot fire and to his side was a pile of stones. He had a large flat stone and a grinding stone. The grinding stone was tied from end to end with wi-go-b to protect his fingers. He put a small stone on the big flat one and then he rubbed the small stone with the grinding stone. He was making arrow tips.

After visiting Uncle Ge-pa-gwa-na-gwa-d, Oona and E-quay went to the lodge of A-wa-sa-si as they did each day. They stood in the doorway with eyes cast down until A-wa-sa-si said, "Enter and sit, my children." The floor was lined with reed mats on which lay a bearskin rug, the only one in the village. This bearskin fascinated the children, but they did not sit on it.

A-wa-sa-si was the oldest person in the new village, as she had been in the old place. She had no children or grandchildren there, for her two sons lived far to the east, but she was considered the Grandmother to all. Because A-wa-sa-si was very old, it was she who told the legends and the history of the people to the children.

Oona and E-quay hoped A-wa-sa-si would speak a lesson or tell them of the old days. They did not expect to hear a legend of Wi-ni-bo-sho, for these legends were told only at the time of the white on the ground. But that day A-wa-sa-si did not speak. She was busy winding wi-go-b. She had balls of the twine before her. When the girls rose to leave, A-wa-sa-si said, "Thank you, my children, for this visit." The older people were always polite to the young people.

When it was time to start the planting, E-quay came for Oona. It was very early dawn, right after the kin-nik-a-nik had been offered for the day. The two girls poked holes in the ground in the many open spaces in the forest. Then On-da-g dropped in the seed. She had saved much seed from the last harvest, so there would be a big crop of pumpkins, squash, beans, and ma-da-min, the corn. It took five dawns before they finished the planting. Then they went to mark the places where the wild food might grow. Throughout the summer the girls went to look at the forest spots. They saw the plants when they first poked through the earth, and they saw the green of the young plants blend with the green of the forest.

In the summer when On-da-g said the time was

right, Oona and E-quay went blueberry picking with Mother, Aunt On-da-g, and the many cousins. The berries were large and many. Before any were eaten, the first berries were offered to the Great Spirit. When the berries were put on birch-bark sheets to dry, Oona and E-quay watched over them, shooing the dogs away. They also had to shoo away the very small children who liked to hear the birch bark crunch beneath their feet.

There were times of rain and thunder. Oona and E-quay did not like these times because they had to stay in their lodges and do the sewing and threading of shells and animal teeth. These were the hard times, the frightening times, when they heard the crashing of A-ni-mi-ki, the thunder, the voice of conflict. But these were also the times when Oona could talk to Father, and this relieved her spirits.

Oona did not see Father often, for he was the ricing leader. It was he who looked for and found the ricing spots, and all through the summer he checked and watched the lakes and rivers. It was he who said the time was right for the harvest. Everyone went to the ricing harvest except A-wa-sa-si, Aunt On-da-g, who was ready to harvest her garden, and Oona and E-quay, who stayed to help with the garden plants and to take wood and food to A-wa-sa-si. Oona did not feel too bad about staying behind because she liked Aunt On-da-g. She knew that she would go next time, for she must learn the ricing as well as the gardening.

The harvesting of the planted seed began. Oona helped pick and stack the squash and pumpkins. After the bean plants were pulled up by the roots and heaped upon the ground, Oona and E-quay threshed the beans by dancing on them. They picked out the beans and put them into muk-kuk-ko-ons-sug. Then the harvesters picked the corn and hung it in the sun to dry. Added to this crop was the wild food which they also dried and stored.

Aunt On-da-g made hominy in the ancient way. She filled a muk-kuk with water and hot ashes and into it dropped a hot stone, removed it, and dropped in another until the ash water was boiling hot and clear. Then she poured the liquid from the ashes. She boiled the corn in this clear ash water until the black centers showed and each kernel was soft. Then she removed the corn from the ash water and boiled it again in clear water until it was fluffy. Finally she burned deer hooves until the hard part fell off. When the inner hooves cooled, she scraped them into the hominy for flavor.

After the garden and rice were harvested and everyone was back in the village, the people held a thanksgiving feast. Rice was offered to the east, south, west, and north, and some was blown on the wind to be carried to the Gitchi Manito. The time had been good and the storing of food for the winter was good. The people had dried fish and stacked the skins of animals for the winter's sewing. They faced the first winter in the new place with contentment and plenty. Oona spent many winter evenings in the lodge of her grandparents, who told her stories with a laugh in their eyes. She learned why the beaver boxed up the water and why the rabbit traded his tail to the chipmunk.

The following year was also a good one, and

Oona went to the sugar bush and the ricing camp. Her life followed the pattern the Ojibway had followed for many years. It was a pleasant cycle and she learned all that young Ojibway girls must know.

It seemed to Oona as if this place had always been her home. She thought, "We are so deep in the forest that the strange people could never touch us." Indeed, the people of the village knew when the strangers were in the forest, but they also knew that the strangers were unaware of them, for the forest was their ally.

Oona Dreams

ONE MORNING in the summer of Oona's seventh year there was a piece of charcoal by her morning meal. She knew the time had come when she must take serious thought of life. She must either pick up the charcoal and go into the forest to learn whether she had a special gift, or she could ignore the charcoal and eat her morning meal. This was the custom of the people, to learn which girls would be Dreamers or Medicine People. Oona sat looking at the charcoal and, being a brave girl, she picked it up and went into the forest.

She walked to the rocky place and down through the meadows filled with flowers. Then she stepped into the pine grove. Her footsteps on the cushion of pine needles and moss made no sound. In the grove the sunlight glowed dimly through the trees. She could not hear the birds sing or the chipmunks chatter, so she moved to where the trees were popple, elm, birch, and evergreen. There she found a sunny spot and sat down to dream.

Oona thought of the many things Ojibway girls did and of the many things she must learn. She thought of Grandfather and Grandmother and how year after year they followed the same pattern of life. Soon she fell asleep. She slept for hours and she dreamed many dreams. When she awoke she was very thirsty and she returned to the village. She had decided what she must do.

She went to Grandfather and Grandmother and told them that in one of her dreams she saw a person, a man standing on a log. Behind him were many faces. They were blurred but they were white. She asked Grandfather what the dream meant and he said, "The time will come when you will know what your dream means."

The summer moved lazily and the sun seemed close to the earth. Many times when it breathed on the earth it was very hot, but many more times the rain fell. The clouds were black with anger, and streaks of lightning sent the trees crashing down. The voice of A-ni-mi-ki thundered.

The harvest was late and the ricing was late. Oona became sad because A-wa-sa-si had asked Father and Grandfather to move her lodge away from the village. They knew that she would spend the days meditating. Her time was soon to come.

After the hunting was over and the white came, the cold was as sharp as the light from the sky in summer. A time of heaviness and dread was with the people.

A-wa-sa-si was ailing and she thought often of her two sons who were far to the east. She wanted once more to see them. In the spring after the maple-sugar time she became very ill, but between her and the long journey was the wish to see her sons.

One evening Oona sat dreaming. It was the same dream. She saw the man standing on the log. She saw other faces behind him. They were blurry and white. But the man on the log had A-wa-sa-si's face. She saw a great river and another river beside it and small gulls overhead. When she awoke she told her mother of the dream. Then Grandfather came and said, "Tell me your dream, my daughter."

So she told him about the dream and the man on the log. That night there was a council. The families met and decided that A-ki-wa-a-si (Old Man), the second son of Grandfather, would go to the place where the big river flowed and he would search for A-wa-sa-si's son.

The next day A-ki-wa-a-si prepared for the long trip and quickly departed. He would travel by canoe through the rainy rivers and lakes. Then he would go south to the country of the Dakota, for that was where the two rivers met.

The corn was planted and harvested. The blueberries were picked and dried, and the people were preparing to go ricing. On the night before they left, Oona dreamed that A-wa-sa-si was smiling and happy. She told this to Grandmother who believed and became happy too. Gazing at Oona, Grandmother knew she was something special.

When the others left for ricing, Mother stayed at the camp to be near A-wa-sa-si. Oona stayed too and she went many times to the lodge of A-wa-sa-si and sat before her. Oona would send her thoughts to A-wa-sa-si and A-wa-sa-si would return her thoughts. "I shall see you smile. I shall see you happy again, A-wa-sa-si."

And A-wa-sa-si said, "Yes, my child, I shall smile again. I shall be happy again, for this is your wish and I know you have dreamed. It is the custom of our people to be guided throughout their lives by their dreams. Some are especially blessed, for their dreams can tell us what will come, what must be, and what we must do.

"I go on a journey, but it will be a good journey, for my life has been full and rich. But I wish to tell you of many things, and these I wish you to tell my grandchildren, whom I have never seen. For you I leave this task.

"The Anishinabe have always been a thriving people born to the woodland way of life. We know the secrets of the forest and receive the gifts of a Generous Spirit. These we repay by honoring and respecting the living things in the forests: the animal people and the plant life which in itself is life-giving. We do not waste the precious gifts, but share them with our brothers.

"Some of us are hunters, some fishermen, some woodsmen, and some planters; but all of us are blessed in the belief that the earth is precious and the spirits of the Animal Brothers clean.

"We make our homes of the forest poles and bark of trees. We have many kinds of lodges and each kind has a purpose. There are the winter lodge, the summer lodge, the sugar lodge, the medicine lodge, and many other small lodges.

"The Animal Brothers have lent their name and power to each family root. This is what we call the do-daim, which means clan. Our people are of the Ma-i-ga-n (Wolf), A-wa-sa-si (Bullhead), and Muk-

kwa (Bear) clans. Members of our do-daim are scattered throughout the places where our people have
lived. We always have a place of welcome in their
lodges.

"We believe in a Great Spirit, and we call Him
Gitchi Manito. All things are carried on the wind to
His presence, and the sun, the moon, and the stars
speak to Him. In dreams He gives the power of the
earth to the Ojibway.

"We honor the earth, for it is our Grandmother,
and its gifts are of our Grandmother. We know our
Grandmother changes her spirits from cold to warm,
from warm to hot, from hot to warm, from warm to
cold. This is her cycle, but with each change she
gives the gifts that are appropriate and necessary.
She is part of the Great Spirit, and we honor her too
when we offer the first fruits of each harvest. We offer kin-nik-a-nik each rising of the sun and offer
thanks to the sun again when it leaves the earth to
speak to the Great Being.

"Our life cycle follows the circle designed by
Grandmother Earth. In the early spring at the time
when the snow turns to water, we go to the sugar
bush and make the maple syrup, the maple cakes,
and the maple sugar. In the warmth of the late
spring, we plant the seed for corn, squash, pumpkin, and beans. In the hotness of the summer, we
pick the berries, starting with strawberries, then pin
cherries, chokecherries, precious blueberries, and
gooseberries. After the blueberry gathering, the harvest begins. The ma-no-min is taken from the lakes,
threshed, and stored along with the corn, squash,
pumpkin, and beans. Throughout the summer the

meat is dried and stored and the herbs and medicine secured. The fish is dried and the acorns hung. The kin-nik-a-nik is scraped and prepared for daily use.

"We believe in the circle of life. We believe that all returns to its source; that both good and bad return to the place where they began. We believe that if we start a deed, after the fullness of time it will return to us, the source of the journey. If care is not used when the circle is begun, then the hurts along the way will be received in the end. Such is the belief of the true Ojibway.

"We believe in the sharing of the harvest and gifts. It is an honor to have the sharing accepted, and it is your joy when the sharing gives joy. This is carried on the winds to the ears of the sun and given to the moon, and thus it is heard by the Gitchi Manito, who gives a larger sharing by your hand.

"Because the earth is our Grandmother and our Grandmother is old, the Old Ones of our do-daim are called grandmothers and grandfathers. Because they are wise and have known Grandmother Earth longer, we hear their words and remember them, for they are the words of the grandmothers and grandfathers who were before us. Thus the young hear what they must teach when they become the Old Ones.

"We believe that the animal people are our brothers and they honor us as such, for each of these brothers gives us something special which he alone possesses. We honor him for this and give his spirit the thanksgiving which is carried on the wind to the ears of the Gitchi Manito. Thus the Ojibway sustain life. Our life and the life of our Animal Brother is one. We give back to the earth life, and thus the circle is complete.

"The children of the Ojibway are the beloved. When they are born they are given a song and a medicine bag by a namer. The first is given in honor to its grandmother and grandfather, the parents of the mother. They cherish the child, teaching and showing the places where footsteps must tread.

"The second, third, and other children are given in honor to a namesake who must watch the growing child and speak to the parents often. Never is a child without the spoken words of the Old Ones.

"The girls must pick up the charcoal at the morning meal to see if they have been given a special power. The boys are given to the vision quest. They gain a feather, a headband, a roach (headdress), a drum, and a pipe only as their prowess grows.

"These are the beliefs of our Ojibway people. We sustain the beliefs, and the beliefs sustain us. That is a circle. From seed to harvest, the life of the Ojibway is full and it is sufficient. This is what must not be lost, and this is what you must tell my grandchildren."

Oona thought to herself, "Yes, A-wa-sa-si, I will do as you say. I shall tell them about you and the many things I have learned from you and the good life you have lived."

The second day after ricing time, when the daylight clashed with the shadows, A-ki-wa-a-si returned. With him was a stranger who had A-wa-sa-si's face. He was dressed in strange clothes. The village welcomed him and took him to A-wa-sa-si's lodge. He said that younger brother would be coming too.

Oona went to the lodge of A-wa-sa-si and stood in the door with eyes cast down. A-wa-sa-si said, "Look at me, my child." She looked at A-wa-sa-si's smiling face, golden with happiness in the fading sunlight. Oona smiled within herself.

That evening the people of the village met. They talked about Oona. A-ki-wa-a-si told them it was just as she had dreamed. A-wa-sa-si's son stood on the logs as they flowed down the river at the place called Ga-ga-yo-sh-ko-ons-i-ca, the place where the small gulls live, in the land of the Dakota. But the land of the Dakota was filled with the strangers with the white faces. The people knew then that Oona was a gifted person who could dream to plan future actions.

Four days after A-wa-sa-si's younger son entered the village, A-wa-sa-si left on her journey and the village was hushed with sadness. Oona felt the loss deeply. She knew that A-wa-sa-si had taught her many of the wise things of life and there was much yet to be learned.

The people honored A-wa-sa-si in the customary way. Her medicine was burned over clean ground. A lock of her hair was cut and put in a small doeskin bag that was placed in a bundle along with her most cherished possessions. This bundle was given to Grandmother to keep during the mourning period. Two mourners, Mother and On-da-g, went to the river and called A-wa-sa-si's name to the other side so that it might be carried to the ears of the ancestors. Then A-wa-sa-si was given to the earth.

The Ojibway believe that one's last journey is made through churning waters. They believe that all animals have spirits larger than themselves. If you wantonly harmed any animals, then their souls would be in the water, churning it so that you might not pass through. If you respected the human and animal brothers, then the journey waters would be quiet. The waters would be quiet for the passing of A-wa-sa-si, for she had been a good person.

The mourning period would last one year, and at the end the people would hold a remembering feast. Then A-wa-sa-si's possessions would be given away and the lock of her hair burned. Every day during the mourning period Oona would think about A-wa-sa-si, repeating to herself the many things that A-wa-sa-si had taught.

The sons of A-wa-sa-si sat around the evening campfires and told the people about the changes in the land of the Anishinabe. They spoke of the strangers who cut the forests and of the logs filling the rivers to the south. They told of the A-sa-bi-ig-go-na-ya, who wore the clothes of nettle fibers, and the Chi-o-ni-ga-mig Anishinabe, the people of the big water – who were few in numbers. During the past cold these people had suffered much hunger and a great coughing sickness. The sons of A-wa-sa-si said that all Ojibway must now live on land designated by a white o-ge-ma, the chief who lived in the land of the Cherokee. All Ojibway leaders had signed a paper and agreed that it must be so.

Grandfather said, "The strangers have not found

this place yet. We will stay for two more ricings, and if the strangers come, then we will go to these places as the chiefs promised."

The sons of A-wa-sa-si left for the land of the small gulls, but they promised to return to let the villagers know about their kinsmen.

The people talked for many days about what A-wa-sa-si's sons had said. They decided to stay until the strangers were very near. The year passed slowly, and always there was an oppressive feeling. They knew that soon they must leave the rainy country.

It was the time of the cold, and the cold came early. Ki-we-di-n, the north wind, played many tricks on the forest people. First he sent the rains slashing at the earth, and then he blew his mighty breath and turned the rains to little balls of ice. He howled and he howled and the whole earth was a hard sheet of water. He howled and howled and the white came and covered up the hard water. He howled and howled and the huge drifts of white piled up against the lodges. But the lodges of the Ojibway faced east and he could not get in.

In the lodge of Oona's father and mother it was warm and cozy. The fire leaped and made patterns on the walls, many patterns and shadows. Oona sat on a robe of beaver skin before the fire. She watched the flames and the pictures that they made, and she began to dream. She woke to the sound of her mother's voice telling her it was time to eat.

"Mother," Oona said, "I have dreamed A-wa-sa-si's son walked into our forest home and with him was a man dressed in the strange clothes and with the pale face. I know they are near, my mother, for I see them when I sleep."

It was all true. When Ki-we-di-n stopped his howling and the sun glistened and made sparkles on the white, A-wa-sa-si's oldest son entered the village. With him came a stranger whose face was as pale as the white that glistened on the ground.

White Earth

THE PEOPLE greeted A-wa-sa-si's son, On-da-bi-tung (Up Step-By-Step), and welcomed the stranger who had traveled with him. They prepared a feast and made a place of rest for them.

After the time of resting, On-da-bi-tung met with the people and said, "I bring the stranger, for he has a paper that must be obeyed. He will read the paper to you and I will tell you what it means."

The stranger read the paper written by the White Father in the land of the Cherokee. The people listened to the strange words.

On-da-bi-tung said the paper meant that they must leave the rainy country and move to a place called a Native Area. The new place would be theirs forever. The Ojibway would live in one part of the forest and the strangers in another, and neither would go into the other's part.

On-da-bi-tung said the village in the rainy country was in the strangers' part of the forest and that was why the people had to move. "Our part of the forest is great," he said, "and there will be room for all. We will be given food, shelter, clothing, and iron kettles."

The people talked back and forth and they said, "It must be so, because On-da-bi-tung has said it is, and we must respect the promises of our o-ge-ma."

They told the stranger they would move when the white turned to water, and he was welcome to stay until then. The stranger said he would stay and when the time came to move, he would show them their part of the forest. This was agreed upon and the kin-nik-a-nik was smoked in the pipe of peace to bind the word.

The white and the cold stayed a long time. The maple-sugar harvest was late, as if the sap in the trees refused to run. And afterward, the flowers did not bloom nor did the leaves appear on the trees. It seemed as if the whole forest refused to watch the passing of the Ojibway from the land.

When the sun warmed the earth and made the water in the rivers and in the lakes flow, the people prepared for the journey. While the men went for the canoes hidden at the small river, two days away, the women prepared the bundles. When all was ready, the people looked at A-wa-sa-si's journeying place and then they left.

They followed the small stream across the meadow and into the birch and popple grove. There the stream grew wider, and the people set off in canoes. They would travel the lakes and rivers to the rising sun.

After two days, the stranger said that they must go over land to the south, but the people wanted to stay on the lakes until a river ran south. This they did. When they had traveled a day and a half on the river, the stranger told them to go west to reach the lakes and the land set aside for the Ojibway. So, carrying their canoes and bundles, they walked west for three days to the Lake of Nettles, which the stranger said belonged to the Ojibway.

They went north on the lake and came to a camp with many, many Ojibway people. They found their kinsmen, their do-daim, who made them welcome.

The stranger took them to another stranger and told him, "These Ojibway have come from the rainy country."

And the second stranger said, "Let them go to the Native Area called White Earth, for I have too many Ojibway here."

Oona and her family knew they must make another journey. They asked On-da-bi-tung, "Where is this other place?"

On-da-bi-tung said, "It is to the setting sun and south."

"How long will the journey take?" asked Oona's father. "We must get there before the ricing time and prepare for the white to come."

On-da-bi-tung answered, "If we follow the rivers, maybe two moons."

So, although the do-daim said, "Stay. The stranger will not remember you, for he does not remember Ojibway faces," the people prepared to leave. They chose Oona's father to lead them, for he was young and strong. He could better understand the strangers and their demands.

The journey from the Lake of Nettles was long and hard. They traveled so many lakes and rivers that Oona was glad for the time of walking between them. The camping times grew longer so they could hunt and gather food. When they passed the lodges of the stranger, their eyes looked only ahead.

A-bo-wi-ghi-shi-g, the old leader, had come with them. He had lost his wife and daughters during the last winter's cold, and now he too became ill. The journey was very hard and he was very old. During the beauty of blueberry time A-bo-wi-ghi-shi-g traveled the river of churning waters to the side where the ancestors stood. He had his pipe, his drum, his feathers, his kin-nik-a-nik, his muk-kuk of wild rice and maple sugar. There was much mourning and sadness, for A-bo-wi-ghi-shi-g had been a good leader.

After the blueberry time Oona and her people reached a place with great numbers of lodges and Ojibway people. They knew it was the White Earth. To Oona it seemed a mixed-up place, for there were many kinds of lodges – round lodges of mats and birch bark, lodges made of forest poles, lodges made of inner wood, and lodges made of cloth. Many of the Ojibway wore the strangers' clothes and lived in the strange lodges.

But the Ojibway were kind. They offered the travelers food and resting places, but the people would not enter the strange lodges. After the resting time, the village leader of this big place took them to a long lodge of inner wood. He said that they must mark a paper before a man called Agent, and afterward they would be given food and clothing.

They all stood ready, but the man called Agent said only the men should mark and tell their names. He did not look at the women and children, but he said, "Tell them to pick a spot."

Father talked to the people and they said, "Let us go deep into the forest. The forest is big. We will find a place before the winter comes." So they left the village of many Ojibway and went two days walking into the forest land. There they made their home. They were late in preparing and storing food, so Father went back to the big place and talked to the ricing leader, who said they could go to a small lake called A-wa-sa-si. Father said, "This is good." When he returned and told the people this, they gave thanks with a small feast.

They made their rice and they hunted and they fished and they dug the wild food. They knew that this time of cold would be hard, for their store of food was little. But they thanked the Gitchi Manito for the good rice harvest and for their Animal Brothers who still lived in the forest.

The winter was indeed long and the food scarce. The deer and the rabbit seemed to have left the land. The men of the village had to go deep into the forest to hunt. Sometimes they were gone for two days, for they did not return until they had the meat for the children to eat.

Oona's father said, "When I travel into the forest to hunt, I will find the maple trees, for we must have a sugar bush." He marked the places he thought would be fine for the maple-sugar camp. When the white was turning to water, he took the people to a group of trees. It was a good maple forest and again they made the maple sugar.

When the warmth hit the earth again, they found the spots to plant the corn and squash and beans. In their second new home, they resumed the yearly cy-

cle of gardening, berry and rice harvesting. After ricing time, Oona and her family group went to the big
place to join the other Ojibway people in a feast to
give thanks for the good harvest. Then they returned
to their new place and settled in for the time of cold.
The second winter there was good. They did not
have the sickness that was in the big place. They
lived much as they lived in the rainy country.

One day Oona said to Mother, "A man will
come," and Mother knew that Oona had dreamed.
Early one morning an Ojibway man dressed in the
manner of the strangers came to their lodges. He
spoke to them respectfully and said his name was
Sam. He had a paper and he read it to them in the
strange tongue. He said it meant that they should
move to the big village, where their children would
go to school. This had been agreed when the leaders made their marks on the treaty paper. The people did not like this, so Sam said that if the people
stayed within their forest, they must send the children to the big village at the time of ricing. They
would live in a longhouse with other Ojibway children and go to school.

The people decided to send one child to the
school with Sam, but to live the winter within their
forest. During the winter white they would decide
what they would do. It was agreed that the second
son of On-da-g, Ma-gi-ghi-shi-g (Starting Sky),
would go. Just before the time of ricing Grandfather
took him to the big village and left him at the school.

The winter was a peaceful time, and it was mild
and short. The people rejoiced and gave thanks, for

the deer and the rabbit had stayed near their village.
The people felt that the short winter was a good sign
and that the planting season would be long and
good.

Through all this time, however, Oona felt a
heaviness in her heart. She said, "Mother, I have not
dreamed. I cannot dream, but I have a feeling here."

Mother said, "They will come, my child. The
dreams will come. Then you will know. It is because
you are fearful now that the dreams do not come.
Look at the trees and the earth around you. Although the strangers are here, our Animal Brothers
and the trees are at peace. Look at them and you will
be at peace too."

So Oona went into the forest. As she sat she
could feel the peace stealing over her. When she
returned to the lodge, Mother said, "Come, my
child, we shall go to the lodge of your grandfather
and your grandmother and there we will talk." So
they went to Grandfather's lodge. Father was there.
Oona sat before them with eyes cast down.

Grandfather said, "Speak, my child, tell us what
you dreamed."

Oona said, "I have seen my mother in the clothes
of the strangers. I have seen a lodge made of the
trees of the forests. I know that this is what my
mother wants."

Mother looked at her daughter and said, "Yes,
this is so. I have thought about this many times. The
strangers and their ways are overtaking us. We cannot live forever in a bark lodge. They want to change
us and I wish to do some of the things, make some
of the changes, so that our children and our grand-

children will not have the difficult life. But I know that even if we accept some of the ways there will always be the clash between our ways and theirs."

Grandfather and Grandmother looked at Oona's mother. They respected her words. Grandfather said, "My daughter, I have known you always to be smiling and I know that lately you have not smiled. Your thoughts have been on other things. I respect your thoughts. I have heard the other Old Ones in the big village speak. They say that we must accept some of the new ways, but we must take only the ways that are good. We must keep what we can and try to remain what we are within our hearts. So if this is your wish, then this is what we will do. We will move to the village and build the strange lodges."

Mother said, "Yes, On-da-bi-tung will visit us soon. Since he knows what the strangers do, we shall ask him about their ways."

When On-da-bi-tung came, they asked him how the trees were cut and how the lodges were built. "You are going to accept the new ways?" he asked. Mother said, "No, we will accept the new lodges, for they will stand longer than the birch bark and the reeds."

On-da-bi-tung said, "I work for the strangers in the big camp and I dance upon the logs in the river. This is how I get a thing called money. With this money you can buy the many things that are necessary." Mother said, "My husband shall go with you and dance on the logs, and he will get the thing called lumber to build the new lodges." So Father went with A-wa-sa-si's son and was gone through the winter and the spring.

During the winter the people planned their new life. Mother, who had always been very quiet, was the one who made the plans. On-da-g came to talk to Mother in the evenings when the children were asleep. Mother said that Oona and E-quay must go to the strangers' school and they must learn the new things. All the Ojibway people would have to make the change. She said that Oona's dream meant that a new way was coming. They must not discard all of the old ways when they accepted the good things from the strangers. Then maybe they would be able to live at peace again.

Mother said, "On-da-g, you will plant the gardens and the children will help. The father of your children should go to the big village and learn to build the strange lodges. His hands have always been clever. He is a maker of things, and in doing this, he will be near your second son. Grandfather and Grandmother will pick the herbs that will keep us well."

Before the time of sugar making the plans were made. Mother said to Oona, "You will go to the school, my child, when we go to the village. You must learn the strangers' language so that we will know what we must face. You have been happy and know only our ways. I know you will remember and teach your children and the other Ojibway children about the goodness we have known."

When Father returned in the early summer he said that the man at the wood camp would give them lumber to build their lodges. "But," said Father, "I must return and work the next cold season and the next after that."

Mother said, "If this is what you must do, then it shall be. We must make the change."

After the evening meal when the forest was still and the children of the village were quiet, Father told Mother what he had learned. "The place where I go is four days walking from here," he said. "It is called a lumber camp. There are many strangers there and also many Ojibway people. It is a strange life, although it is not difficult. On-da-bi-tung and I push and pull a thing called a saw across the bottom of the tree until the tree falls. After many trees have fallen, we cut off the branches. We pile the trees on a thing called a wagon and this is pulled by animals called oxen. These animals have the body of a buffalo and horns that curve.

"When the white turns to water, the fallen trees are put into the river. Then On-da-bi-tung and I dance on them so they do not jam. We travel this way down the rivers and lakes until we reach a place where the trees are split into the pieces called lumber, the thing that you want.

"I do not like cutting the trees," said Father. "I think too often of the animal people. They will be few, and they will be gone from this land. When we have enough of the lumber, I shall no longer cut the trees or travel the rivers on them. My heart cries too often when I do this."

"My heart, too, cries often," said Mother. "It cries because we are surrounded. The strangers who cut the trees are many and now the people who do the

planting are here. And my heart cries for the Ojibway children who will never feel the moss beneath
their feet or look up at the shi-n-go-b, the tall trees,
as Oona has done.

"Also," said Mother, "after Grandfather sprinkles
the kin-nik-a-nik in the early morning, he and
Grandmother sit within the lodge. They seldom
speak now. Their eyes have a waiting look. It is as
if they see that which is beyond the sky."

Oona, who was listening, felt the tears come.

Mother told Father about the sickness that was in
the big Ojibway village. "At maple-sugar time," she
said, "we met some kinsmen from the big village
who told us of the things that have happened and of
the many Ojibway who have made the last journey.
They said that the food promised to them by the
great chief does not come and there has been much
hunger. We must plan," said Mother. "We will accept the strange lodges and the things that go
within, but we must do the things we have always
done, for they are still necessary."

"Tomorrow," said Father, "we shall go to the big
village to see what has happened during the time of
cold. I wish to talk to the Old Ones there, for they
must not depend on the strangers' ways. They must
again grasp the old ways to show our people how to
survive."

"We will take On-da-g with us so she may get her
son from school," said Mother. "Oona will come and
maybe E-quay also, for Oona would like to have her
along."

The next day Father called the people together.

He told them that they must all agree either to move to the big Ojibway village or to stay in their forest place.

The people were afraid of the sickness in the big village. Every time of cold the sickness was there. "We have been favored," they said, "because we did only what we have always done." They did not want to leave the old place. Father said, "If this is your wish, then we will stay."

Grandfather said, "Each ricing time the man will come for the children. If they live in the longhouse of the school they will never know our ways. Our strength will be lost. If we move close to the big village, the children will stay home at night and we can still teach them the old ways. We must decide — shall we stay separate and not see the children from ricing to planting, or shall we speak to them each night about the good of our people?"

The people said, "We shall go to the big village."

Father said, "It shall be. Some of us will stay here and gather the berries and others will go to the new place. If things go well, we shall all be in the new place before the ricing."

New Homes, Old Ways

FATHER, MOTHER, On-da-g, Oona, and E-quay went to tell the man called Agent that they would be part of the big Ojibway village and that they wished to have their share of the land. Agent said, "Take your pick." So the families chose a spot that was quite removed from the other lodges, near a tiny stream.

"This is where we will build our lodges," said Oona's mother.

Oona looked at the new place and said, "Yes, Mother, I have dreamed of this place. I have dreamed that in this part of the big Ojibway village we would live and there would be eight lodges."

Mother said, "But there are only six families."

Oona said, "In my dream I saw eight lodges."

Mother said, "Then it must be so, if this is what you dreamed."

They set up the temporary lodges with the birch bark. These would do, Mother said, until the wood called lumber came. Then they would start building the strange lodges.

On-da-g went to the school and told the Ojibway helper, "I want my son home for a little while." The agent said to his helper, "Tell her to take him, but he

must be back before the time of ricing." So On-da-g's
second child came home for the summer. And indeed the rest of the families were very much aston-
ished, for he could speak the strangers' language.

Mother said, "This is good. You must speak to
the strangers for us when On-da-bi-tung is not
here."

On-da-g's son told them that in the language of
the stranger he was called David. He said the strangers had a practice of having two names. The second
one was for all of those in the family, but the first
names were all different. He said the strangers at the
school called him David and he himself had chosen
a last name, Green, for the color of the forests. In the
language of the strangers, all the people in their small
band would have the last name of Green. He said he
did not know why the strangers did this, but it was
so. Many Ojibway people had names in the strange
tongue.

Father talked to the other leaders in the village,
and at a council the leaders said, "We must not rely
on the strangers' promise of food. Instead we must
plant and gather the gifts of the forest so that again
we will be strong."

They stayed three weeks in the big village. When
the wagon with the lumber did not come, Mother
said, "We will return to the small forest village and
we will stay until we learn that the wagon has come.
And Father, you must come too."

They went back to the small village and planted
and harvested just as before. But one day On-da-bi-
tung came with a stranger.

Father said, "I know that stranger. He is the man

from the big camp, the one who cut the trees."

On-da-bi-tung said to Father, "The man wishes you to come back and help with the new logs that have been cut."

Mother said to Father, "You will not go back until we learn what has become of the trees called lumber."

On-da-bi-tung told the stranger this, and the stranger said that he would pay Father the money with which he could buy the lumber for the house.

Mother said to Father, "This we will not do. This man must give you the lumber as he promised."

On-da-bi-tung told the stranger this. The stranger said, "Very well, I agree."

Mother said to Father, "Then you will go back, but the lumber must be here at the next planting time. So again we must spend the coming cold here in this small village, and it will be as it was before."

Before the ricing time, a man called Soldier came to their little village. David spoke to him, then told the people that again it was time for him to go to school. But the man wanted the other children in school too. Grandfather said that since they must make the change, it should be so. The families had a council and decided that two of the sons and the daughter of Father's third brother would also go.

Grandfather said to Oona's mother, "I shall take the children and walk with the soldier. I shall stay until the children are settled at the longhouse."

And Mother said to Grandfather, "Then bring us the kettles the agent has promised." And to David she said, "Tell the agent we wish to have these kettles. They must be brought to us by Grandfather."

When Grandfather returned he had two of the iron kettles. Mother said, "We shall see if it is as David said, that these kettles will boil the food without dropping in the hot stones."

When they went to the ricing camp, Mother saw other Ojibway people using huge muk-kuk-ko-ons-sug called barrels to parch the rice. She was determined that they must also acquire these things.

The winter passed quickly. It was as if Grandmother Earth wished them to hurry on to the new life. After the maple-sugar time and before the time of planting, Mother said to On-da-g, "We will go to the big village and we will do our planting there. We will build the temporary shelters. I know it should be so, for Oona has dreamed of the eight lodges again. Grandmother and Grandfather will come with us, and you must bring your family, too."

When the flowers were bright with sunlight, the two families packed their bundles and their clothing. They looked at the old place and knew that this time they would not return.

When they reached the big Ojibway village to prepare the place for their lodges, they found much sorrow. The Ojibway people there had suffered much through the winter. The wagonloads of food and clothing promised by the big leader again had not arrived. There had been much hunger. The children were weak and thin, and many had the coughing sickness. There were faces missing, for many had made the last journey. The people in the big village told them that they were foolish to move, that they were better off in the tiny village deep within the forest. But Mother was determined to make the change. She said to the people, "We shall stay."

On-da-g went to get her son from the school. David told his mother of a stranger who lived on a place called a farm. He wanted David to stay the summer to help him build fences and lodges for the animals.

David said, "I am a man now, my mother. I am fourteen years, and I am big and strong. I know that I can learn to do the things that the man wishes me to do."

Mother said to On-da-g, "Your son is like his father, who is also a builder. Your husband was the maker of things in our old village and we will need someone to build the new kind of lodges. Do you not think it would be wise for him to go with David to the place called farm and learn the building of the lodges?"

On-da-g talked to her husband, who agreed, "Yes, it would be the wise thing to do. No more will the Ojibway need the many things that I know how to build." So father and son left for the place called farm.

The people built temporary lodges on their chosen site. They prepared to live as they had in their forest home.

Mother said, "This summer we cannot have the big garden that Oona dreamed about, for the trees must be pulled up. We will plant around them in three or four small gardens."

On-da-g said, "I will find the spots."

An Ojibway man called Tom came and said to Grandfather, "I will help your daughters with their planting. I will go to the agent and get the plow, and he will help me to get a horse. It will be easier for them that way."

Grandfather told the daughters and they agreed. They told the man called Tom they did not wish to cut the trees, so they had chosen three spots for their garden. The man tore up the earth around the trees with the plow, and the women went behind and cleared the brush that was left. Then On-da-g, Mother, Oona, and E-quay planted the seed.

When they had finished, Mother sent a message to the other people of their small village. They must come after the berry harvest, for soon Father and On-da-bi-tung would be there with the lumber for the new lodges.

Mother said to On-da-g, "I am going to Agent's lodge to see what kinds of new things are within. Oona and E-quay will go with me, and I will ask David to speak for us."

When the agent understood what Mother wanted, he took her, Oona, and E-quay to his lodge and said to his woman, "This person is curious and would like to see the inside of our house. You might as well include the two young ones too. Maybe it will start them learning civilized ways."

They entered the strange lodge and saw the things within. When the agent realized Mother's interest, he called for his helper and interpreter, an Ojibway man named Dan.

"Tell this woman that if she wishes to help my woman within our lodge she will learn the things she is so curious about. Tell her she must come every day. My woman will show her what to do."

Mother, after seeing the agent's woman, agreed. She said to Oona, "The woman does not look harmful, and this would not be a bad thing to do. I will learn some useful new ways, which I could teach to our sisters, and you and E-quay must go to school to learn the new ways."

So every day Mother went to the agent's lodge and helped the strange woman there. She learned to sew and to make the fire in a thing called a stove. She learned about the table and the chairs and the dishes. Slowly she learned the language of the strangers. She understood the words before she could speak them. In the evening when she returned to the new camp she told On-da-g, "We shall have some of these things. The agent's wife will have the trading man bring what I want.

"But let us keep the old ways too. You must take the children and go into the woods to pick the berries and dry them for the winter as we have always done. And Grandfather and Grandmother must gather the herbs and the medicines necessary to keep us well."

Mother worked very hard. Many times when Oona and E-quay walked past the agent's lodge the day after the strangers' Prayer Day, they saw her bent over a large tin muk-kuk rubbing clothes up and down. Often they went to the stranger's lodge, and Mother showed them how to iron and how to cook.

Mother brought goods home to make dresses and shirts. The girls learned to sew. E-quay was especially interested and she became very clever with the needle.

The agent's wife was a kindly woman who did many of the sharing things that had been part of their old life, things such as taking food to the needy and sick. She made it easier for the people to obtain the new necessities of life. She did not cheat and she became angry when some of her people did so. Because she was as she was, her lodge was filled with the gifts of ma-no-min, maple sugar, and birch bark. The villagers said that she would make a good Ojibway person. Her lack of knowledge about the old Ojibway life made her different, but they respected her, for she lived by her beliefs in the rightness of life.

Before the time of cold, the strange new lodges were up. They were small but well built, for Ge-pa-gwa-na-gwa-d, On-da-g's husband, had learned easily. They were made of sturdy studs and thick, crude lumber with tar paper on the outside walls, overlapping sheets of tar paper on the roof, and heavy planks for floors. The doors faced east, and there was a window in each wall. The chairs, beds, and tables that Ge-pa-gwa-na-gwa-d made were equal to those made by any of the strangers. Soon his products were highly prized and in demand, just as his tools had been in the old life.

Many people from the big village had helped build the lodges, and Oona was happy to talk to the other Ojibway girls. From them she learned about sewing patterns, pins, and mail-order catalogs. Even Grandfather and Grandmother were stirred when the young people stopped at their lodge to wish them well. It pleased them to see that these young people who were so familiar with the strangers' customs also followed the old way, keeping their eyes cast down when talking to the Old Ones.

At the feast and dance after the building, the people talked of the old customs. There was a happy feeling in the air when they offered kin-nik-a-nik and the first rice to the Gitchi Manito. They gave thanks for the gifts of the forest and for the good harvest. For a while they forgot the strangers and their new ways. It was as if there were only Ojibway people in the land once again.

O-Gitchi Da, the Talk Dance, was for the very old Ojibway. Each elder danced his favorite dance and then stopped to talk, most often speaking about the past, about the animal people, about the goodness of life, and from where it comes. Thus did the elders pass on the customs and the history of the do-daim.

The young people glowed with pride as they listened to the Old Ones. They would remember what they had heard, for the air was filled with the spirit of the Ojibway.

Oona listened and her heart filled with joy. She felt that this new place would be a good place. There had been only kind words spoken. Good thoughts and the spirit of giving were there.

Before long the peoples' new lodges held a mixture of the old and the new. Pictures of the Christian life hung on the walls and birch-bark containers and reed mats hung from the rafters. Braided rugs lay on the scrubbed wooden floors, and clothes of gingham and muslin hung on nails near the beds. The buckskin shirts and dresses were packed in trunks and used only for the times of ceremony.

The trees were cut and the land was plowed for the new way of the planting. Oona and E-quay started school after the ricing. Oona felt deeply that this time the change was final.

The new place was named Greenwood by David, and soon everyone called it Greenwood Village. There were seven houses, for On-da-bi-tung had joined the six families. He brought with him a wife who came from the place where the small gulls fly. She was named Charlotte, but she was soon called Aunt Sha-nood. She had two children, a boy and girl whose eyes were gray and whose skin was light. They were baptized and had the Christian names of Peter and Mary. They were good in manner and they respected the Ojibway ways. Peter and Mary could speak three tongues – the English, the language of the voyageurs, and the good Ojibway.

Oona, E-quay, and Mary soon became the best of friends. Together they watched over the smaller children, picked the chips for the morning fires, and carried the water from the pump. And together they paid respects to the Old Ones in the evening.

Aunt Sha-nood taught the new arts that were good. She taught Oona and E-quay to knit and bake. She taught Mother to can food and to speak the English language.

The first winter in Greenwood was good. The harvest had been rich, and the people had gathered and stored much wild food. They had kept all the ceremonies of offering and giving thanks. They had tossed kin-nik-a-nik from the doors each morning. Their greeting to each morning sun had been truthful, and their request to the setting sun sincere.

In the big village the hunger had not been hovering, for the people had harvested well. They had not depended on the pay party of the white chief. But the coughing sickness was there, and the people went to the Mi-de-wi-wi-n to get the herbs that would help. They offered their respect to the healers and the old ways. This angered the agent, who wished to outlaw the Mi-de-wi-wi-n.

Father and On-da-bi-tung went to the agent to explain that the Mi-de-wi-wi-n had a special knowledge of healing, that its members were good people – very good Ojibway people – and that their wisdom was a gift to be respected. This angered the agent even more. He said the Mi-de-wi-wi-n was heathen, and he threatened to charge the people with disturbing the peace. The soldiers were put on the alert, and the people practiced the herb healing in secret. The will of the Ojibway was one again and the tie to the old ways was strengthened.

But always there was the sorrow that the sickness brought, and life was shortened by it. Many times the sickness took mothers and fathers. The children who were left behind were raised as little brothers and sisters by those for whom they were namesakes.

Bitter could have been the thoughts of the Ojibway, but their gift of believing in brotherhood was strong, and their offerings of sharing were a comfort to those who were unable to grasp the new ways.

The elders and leaders of the Ojibway met often in the big village. They talked of the white chief's promises never kept, of the hunger and the sickness. They knew that they alone could keep their people together and help them face the new restrictions.

They set up a self-sufficient pattern of living that kept many of the old customs and beliefs despite the pressure from the strangers.

The gathering of ma-no-min, the blueberry picking, and the making of maple sugar remained satisfying ties with the past. During those times the people camped out and their children were close to the pattern of living that had been the Ojibway way for years before the strangers came.

The Old Ones were honored with gifts of food and clothing, and their words were respected. Their lodges filled with the children and young people who wished to hear the legends and the history of the people. The kin-nik-a-nik was tossed from the doors each morning, an offering to the Gitchi Manito. The songs, the drums, and the dances would not be forgotten.

The New Ways

IT WAS SPRING again. The shallow brook that ran by the houses filled to the brim with melted ice and snow. It bubbled merrily as it ran over the rocks.

Oona stood in the icy brook. She gazed dreamily into the water but saw only the sky and trees. The reflections helped her forget the present and feel the peace and security of the near past. Suddenly she saw her mother's face in a dream. It was harsh and unsmiling. Her eyes were full of anger and yet she seemed to be weeping.

Oona snapped out of her dream and ran quickly to the house. As she entered the side door her mother turned, smiled, and said, "Yes, my daughter?"

The look of tenderness and love in her mother's face quieted Oona's rapidly beating heart. She replied, "I have returned early from school."

"Why is that, my daughter?"

"Many other children did so, too," said Oona. "The forest called, the air in school is bad, and the teacher, also, was anxious to get away."

"How was the school today, my daughter?"

"I learned my lessons, I did the reading and

91

writing, but sometimes I do not like what the teacher says," replied Oona.

"What is that, my daughter?"

"Our old life is bad. We must heed only what we hear in school to make us better people."

Oona saw her mother stiffen.

"What else does the teacher say, my daughter?"

"That the Mi-de-wi-wi-n people are bad and we must shun them," replied Oona. "And that we must become Christian and be baptized."

Oona watched her mother's face tighten; she could scarcely hear her low reply. "I have told the agent's wife we would do these things. I shall talk to your father."

Oona saddened as a look of sorrow crossed her mother's determined face. But she sensed the feelings in her mother's heart—the regret at putting aside the old beliefs and the decisions that made it necessary to accept the new ways.

Oona said softly, "Yes, Mother, we shall do as you say."

That evening Oona went to her grandparents' house. She stood with eyes cast down and with the unsmiling expression.

Grandfather said, "My little daughter, you have come with a troubled heart. Would you speak of this to us so we may help?"

"Yes, Grandfather, I thank you and I do wish to speak," replied Oona. "Grandfather, I have seen my mother's face many times in my dreams. It is harsh and yet it has a weeping look. I feel a disturbance within her. She does not hum softly as she used to do, nor does she smile. Each time I see her face in my dreams, the skin seems more tight over the bones."

"My daughter," said Grandfather, "there is a conflict within your mother. She has accepted the tools of the strangers that in time will replace the tools of the Ojibway. And it may be that the Ojibway people yet to come will know only the new tools. They are but things, and it does not hurt to have them if they are not first over the goodness of the heart. But the old beliefs and goodness of our life will be much harder to deny or trade for what is offered by the strangers."

"My mother says we shall be baptized and become Christians," replied Oona.

"Only time will tell if this is the right thing for our people," said Grandfather. "If it is, then the people who wish us to be baptized will some day come to know the goodness that has been our life. Your mother will know what is good about the new ways, for she herself is a good person. I shall speak to her and perhaps her tumult will cease."

Grandfather looked at Oona with the special look and she felt well and comforted.

Father, Mother, and Oona were baptized and Oona began learning the Christian teachings. They confused her, and on her evening visits to Grandfather and Grandmother she told them so.

"They tell us of a Gitchi Manito," said Oona. "They have a book about him. He is the ruler of all things. He made the earth, the sun, the stars, the moon, and we should know this ruler."

"Yes, my daughter, this is true," said Grand-father. "We know that the Gitchi Manito has given us many gifts."

"Also, Grandfather, they say 'Honor thy father and thy mother.' "

"This is also true, my daughter. I have done this when I was but a child, and I know that you have always done so. Is there something else?"

"Yes, they say 'Love thy neighbor as thyself.' Is this not the brotherhood that we are taught?"

"Yes, my child, we believe in the brotherhood of the people and the animal people. What is it that confuses you?"

"They say we must forget what was taught by our people and we must believe only what we learn now at the church. If it is the same, are not both to be believed?"

"Yes, my child. I can see why it is confusing. They do not know what we believe and they will not learn what we believe. If they did, it would indeed be much easier. But you must remember all the good our people have known and taught. Compare it to what you are now learning. Do not be ashamed of the good that we have taught and do not be ashamed of the good to be learned. Our way of life is chang-ing, and there is much we must accept. But let it be only the good. And we must always remember the old ways. We must pass them on to our children and grandchildren so they too will recognize the good in the new ways."

It is the belief among the Ojibway that when a girl changes into a woman she has a great power for good or evil. So it is the custom that at the very first time — and only the first time — a young girl has the physical signs of change, she must go into the forest, build a ba-ca-ne-ge, a small lodge for herself, and fast. There she will stay for a period of ten days, or as long as she can. During this time she has no contact with anyone. She will neither leave the lodge for a long period of time nor go very far from it. The longer she fasts, the clearer will be her dreams of what she will do in life. If she is a Dreamer or a Medicine Person, her visions will confirm this.

Oona and E-quay had their time in the ba-ca-ne-ge. They built their little wigwams close together, for the time for them was the same. They went to please Grandmother, who had counseled them to go. Grandmother felt strongly that the change from childhood to womanhood must be done with purity and fasting to show that the young woman could overcome the temptations of life.

Because the agent's wife opposed the custom, they did not stay for ten days, but they did have the time of meditation and the beauty of isolation. Even though they had become Christians, Oona and E-quay felt they should honor the customs of the old Ojibway life, and they felt sorrow when these ways were called heathen. They could remember the beauty of that life as it was without the conflicts of the new.

Yes, Oona's pattern of life was changing. There was now the intrusion of school and church. She lived in a house made of lumber and tar paper, just as many other Ojibway families did. She used the tables, chairs, bed, and dishes. Her family, like other Ojibway people, bought the grain and seed from the trading store. But there was much good in Oona's busy life.

Oona still went with Grandmother into the forest to pick the herbs and she went with On-da-g and Sha-nood to cut the birch bark. She helped to plant and weed the gardens with E-quay and Mary during the early morning hours. In the afternoons they still roamed the woodlands picking strawberries, choke-cherries, pin cherries, and raspberries. But now the girls carried the berries in a galvanized syrup pail in-stead of a muk-kuk and spread them on sheets of canvas instead of the birch bark to dry in the sun. But they still had to keep the young ones and the dogs away.

Grandmother, out of habit, still collected the wi-go-b from the basswood tree and the spruce root. She still made the glue from hooves and the gum of trees. Mary, who was new to the knowledge of the old ways, was now Grandmother's constant com-panion on her journeys into the forest.

Now there were pin-cherry and chokecherry jam, waxed rutabagas and carrots, Mason jars for can-ning, and salted fish. These things were adopted from the strangers' culture.

The life of the Ojibway changed in other ways, too. There were many people from the east who came to the towns of the reservations to see the In-dians, and they wanted mementos. So the elders of the village would sit in the sun, cutting birch bark to make owls, birdhouses, and miniature canoes. Sometimes they made patchwork quilts. Whenever they could, Oona, E-quay, and Mary were happy to sit with the Old Ones, to fetch and carry, and to help with the tasks that made it easier for the Old Ones to do the old crafts and use the new tools.

Grandmother and Mother, who had been the weavers in the old life, also made things for the strangers. They had woven fishtraps and mats from the reeds and cattails. They had spun the nettle fiber dresses. Now they applied the old skills to new materials. They wove colorful belts of yarn and braided rugs of rags. But they also did the weaving of willow and sweet-grass baskets.

In the evening, Mother, On-da-g, and Sha-nood would make headbands, belts, and necklaces of beadwork. Oona watched them string the bright beads and lace them across the thread. They used the traditional pattern of most Ojibway women: a colorful flower on a stem outlined by leaves of green.

There were stores in the white man's town where visitors bought the crafts at a high price. Although the price given the Ojibway people was low, the making of their crafts helped them remember the old skills and respect the gift of the birch bark.

The many changes in the Ojibway material life did not change their traditional way of sharing. There was a kindness in the people and in the help they gave to those in distress. Mother, On-da-g, and Sha-nood formed a little society. They sat with the sick and bereaved, and they met to help each other learn the new things that were necessary.

The people also practiced the traditional system of offering to others, holding an honoring feast for a needy or bereaved family. They spread a blanket on the earth and on it heaped gifts of clothing, bead-work, venison, wild rice, maple sugar, wild duck, game, and fish. Beside those products of the old life they placed the new things: dress goods, yarn, nee-dles, thread, tools, seeds, and the new foods. They offered the gifts to the family with the words, "Will you honor us by accepting these gifts?" Then there were speeches praising the good things the family had given to others and their many contributions to the do-daim.

Father and the other men of the big Ojibway village built a roundhouse of logs where the people gathered in the winter to do the traditional dances: the Friendship Dance, the Talk Dance, the Gift Dance, and the Rabbit Dance. The people wore the deerskin, the moccasins, and the roaches — the clothes made the old way with deer hair, tanned hide, and porcupine quills. Ojibway people from other villages came and gifts were exchanged. For the Gift Dance, Ba-ghi-gi-ge-win, a gift such as a blanket, costume, headband, moccasins, or food was given to someone in the village for outstanding works or deeds. To Oona there was an excitement in listening to the drums and bells.

There was much anticipation in the Ojibway vil-lages the summer of Oona's fourteenth year. A run-ner had come to announce that the pay party would be at the big village in two weeks. The agent sent word that all Ojibway people in his custody could come and sign their names. As soon as possible the Ojibway families went to the big village.

It was a time of social greeting. Do-daim visited

do-daim. Oona met many of her kinsmen and made
many new friends. There were merry-making and
matchmaking, foot races and games. On-da-bi-tung
had a moccasin game, and he also taught many of
the Ojibway men the playing of cards. At night the
people danced the Friendship and Talk dances. For
this special gathering the people wore their best, and
the many-colored costumes interested Oona. The
older Ojibway dressed in the old fibers and deerskin,
but some of the younger women had the jingle
dresses made of velvet and rolled tin. Oona wore a
deerskin dress decorated with porcupine quills.

When the pay party arrived, the Ojibway lined
up to sign their names or make their marks. Only the
adult men were allowed to sign, so only they and
their families were counted and paid. Because the
Ojibway knew that this was how they would be allotted, many of the men included widowed women
and their children in their family groups so they, too,
would be counted and paid. Often members of the
pay party thought that the Ojibway men had many
wives.

When the payment was over the people received
their rations – the promised food that seldom came.
Oona looked at their portion – the salt pork, the
beans, the small amount of flour – and she said to
her mother, "It is well that we plant and harvest and
hunt, for this food given us by the White Father
would not be enough."

Her mother said, "Yes, it is well that your father
brings us plenty of meat, and it is well that our crops
are good."

While all the people were still gathered in the big

village, David, who was now seventeen years in age, came to say good-bye. He told the people of Greenwood that he would be going with the pay party to read the words of the white men to the Ojibway in the other Native Areas.

Shortly after the pay party had left and Oona and her family had returned to Greenwood, the agent's helper, Dan, appeared with a very old Ojibway woman and three small children. He told Father that they were the grandchildren of A-wa-sa-si's youngest son. The old woman was the grandmother of the children on their mother's side. The people made them welcome and built them a house. Thus Oona's dream of eight lodges came true.

Mi-n-di-mo-ye (Old Lady), told them that the children had been given in namesake to Father, Mother, and On-da-g, so they became Oona's two sisters and brother. This pleased her very much, for she had always felt different being the only child in her family when there were many children in the other Ojibway families.

But the event that touched Oona most deeply that summer concerned her sister-of-life, E-quay. She knew that E-quay had been feeling womanhood for a long time and that in the eyes of a young man called Walter Horn, E-quay was pretty enough to be spoken for. It was only a matter of time before the families would feast together and E-quay would be leaving for a life of her own.

Walter, a man as old as David, had already tilled some land and planted in the white man's way. He also worked in the lumber camps. Because he had the blood of the voyageurs, he knew many of the strange ways. But he was acceptable for he respected the Ojibway life.

It was late summer. The gardens had been growing fast and clean. On-da-g, Oona, E-quay, and Mary planned one afternoon to pick the medicine plants and dig the sour root, but the leaves on the popple trees had turned with the wind and the day was fast becoming black. They knew a storm was coming and that the rain would last until the time of the sunset. They decided to sew dresses. Later in the week would be a dance, a white man's dance, and this they wished to see.

As they sewed, Oona thought and dreamed. "The people in our lodges are few. The young men are cutting down the trees, working for the strangers. They move deep into the forests to do this work and they take their families with them. Many of the girls like E-quay marry the sweat-lodge strangers. They are taken away and we never see them again." In her dream she saw E-quay wearing a happy, secret smile.

Suddenly E-quay said to her mother, "I shall go with Walter after the ricing time."

On-da-g said, "Yes, Walter has spoken to your father in the old way."

The marriage of Walter and E-quay took place in the church. The agent's wife arranged it in the way of the strangers.

Oona Becomes
a Woman

IN THE FIFTEENTH year of Oona's life, the winter cold cut into her heart. The coughing sickness was bad among the Ojibway and Mother caught it. Her face was tight over the bones, and her body lost the flesh. All winter long On-da-g and Oona sat with her. On-da-g fed her the broth of fish heads to ease her pain. They put hot rocks at her feet to keep her warm and make the sweat come, but her eyes told them that she had lost her spirit. Father sat with Mother also, and Oona saw the look of loss on his face.

In the middle of one dark, dark night Oona was awakened by On-da-g's voice saying over and over, "Ga-wi-n Mi-shi, Ga-wi-n Mi-shi," which meant "Not yet, not yet." Oona knew her mother had left on her journey.

The Christians came to bury Mother, and all through the funeral On-da-g clung to Oona with a dazed and bewildered air about her. Back in Green-wood after the funeral, Oona took On-da-g to her house because she seemed so dispirited and forlorn. On-da-g just sat rocking. Oona suddenly realized how much Mother had meant to On-da-g. Mother had been the strong one; she had talked and On-da-g had always listened, she had planned and On-da-g had always done what was planned. On-da-g had taken the new things when Mother had; she and her family had been baptized when Mother, Father, and Oona had been baptized.

Looking at On-da-g as she sat rocking with the tears silent in her eyes, Oona knew that she would have to help her as Mother had. She said, "On-da-g, now you shall be my mother, and we will have to plan together those things that must be done."

And it was so. Like her mother Oona lent her strength to On-da-g and helped Grandfather and Grandmother understand those new ways that were distasteful to them. She studied carefully the new ways and chose those that would be suitable for their family group, because the uncles and aunts expected it. She was a Dreamer and her power was respected.

Throughout the rest of the winter Father was silent. He did not laugh or joke or even smile. His eyes had a faraway look and seldom did he speak or leave the lodge. He wore his hair long over his face in the old mourning way. When the snow melted and turned to water he said to Oona, "My daughter, it is soon the planting time, and you have much food yet, so I shall go to the lumber camp to find A-wa-sa-si's son, On-da-bi-tung. We shall grow old together. I shall be back with him, for he has been gone a long, long time." Father then went to each of the lodges in Greenwood and sat in silence before the family members. After he left the village, the people smoked the pipe together. Oona, with a crying heart, wrapped her father's pipe, kin-nik-a-nik bag, drum, and bowie knife in a bundle to await his return. She knew that Father was reaching for Mother.

The summer at Greenwood was quiet and heavy. The berries were picked, the crops harvested, and the ma-no-min brought to shore. Grandfather and Grandmother often walked to the prairie's edge and looked at the hills beyond.

Grandmother Earth was angry. She sent rains slashing down and thundering voices. Streaks of lightning cracked the skies and afterward balls of fire rolled over the earth.

Before the first snow fell, On-da-bi-tung brought Father home. He was buried next to Mother in the Christian burial ground.

Oona went into the forest and slept beneath the trees. She listened for the si-si-gwa-d, but could not grasp its sound. She wept then slept again, and in the morning the sun bathed her in warmth. The geese honked overhead, the squirrels chattered, and the sparrows chirped. The wind blew and the leaves rustled. Then Oona sat and dreamed. She saw Father and Mother again smiling beside the lodges in the rainy country. The circle was around them. When Oona awoke, she heard the si-si-gwa-d. It had a weeping sound.

Oona went to Grandfather's and Grandmother's house. Grandfather said, "Tell me, my daughter, what it is you wish to know."

Oona said, "It is my mother. She never spoke about her family or her home. I do not know from whence she came. I wish to know. I have always thought her to be different."

"It is so, my daughter. Her past is silent and there is much that I do not know. I can tell you how she came to us. When we lived far to the rising sun I went one morning to see my rabbit snares, and deep within the forest I found your mother. She was cold, shaken, and frightened. With her was a small, walking child and a woman. Both were dead. We buried the child and woman and brought your mother home. We do not know if the child was hers or the other woman's. We never asked her and she did not tell us. Only once did she speak of her past, and that was when your father and she became one. She said she had lived on the Chi-si-bi and that she was of the Muk-kwa clan. It is not much that I can tell you except that your mother had suffered and that she was a good person.

"My daughter, the journeys of your father and mother surely have been good, for they were good people, good Ojibway. They honored us, the old people. They loved you and the others, and they respected the animal people. They will pass through the turbulent waters safely. They faced a troubled time of change, and they have prepared you for it. Your grandmother and I wait to make the long journey, but before we do, we shall see your children and touch their heads."

In her seventeenth year, Oona married a man whom she had known at school. He was only part Ojibway. His name was A-wa-sa-si-s (Little Fisher), but in the other language he was called Michael. He was a Christian and a farmer and he lived east of the reservation on the Straight River. When Oona moved to A-wa-sa-si-s' farm, she took with her On-da-g, Uncle Ge-pa-gwa-na-gwa-d, their two small grandsons, Grandfather, and Grandmother.

E-quay, who had moved to another part of the reservation when she married, returned to Green-wood with four small children. Her husband had been lost among the logs on the river. Oona brought her to the farm, and she and her children became part of Oona's life again.

In fact, the farm became many with people and with the Animal Brothers who sought refuge there. It was a new kind of life, for since the death of Wal-ter, A-wa-sa-si-s was the only Ojibway who farmed in the white man's way. But it was a good life for Oona and the others. Although the practice of rais-ing the cattle, the horses, and the chickens was alien to them, they were good at the planting of food and harvesting. Through it all they kept the customs and beliefs. They continued the practices of the old life.

It was good to have E-quay back, for she too had helped her husband farm. She had learned much about the harvesting of food, the canning, and the threshing. She was a very good seamstress and was asked many times to make a dress or shirt. One only had to point to a picture in the catalog. E-quay could make the pattern, choose the material, measure, cut, and sew, and the person had the dress that she wanted. It was E-quay who made the weekly visits to the reservation village. She would hitch the horses to the wagon and would leave to do her buying. She took the people to the sugar bush and ricing camps. She also did the work that On-da-g had once done.

Now On-da-g had that way of looking back and listening to the trees. It was good that E-quay could
give her strength.

Oona was so busy with the farm work that she
had little time to meditate, so her powers as a
Dreamer lay dormant. It was only after the harvesting that she could do other things. Her husband,
A-wa-sa-si-s, liked to go trapping every year, and in
this second autumn of her marriage Oona insisted on
going along.

It was the year 1879. The Ojibway in Minnesota
had all been enrolled and contained on reservations,
but to the west and south the Dakota had been
frightening the settlers. Three years before there had
been fighting at Little Big Horn, and the battle still
flamed in the minds of the strangers. It was not a
time for Indians to be too far from their reservation
homes. Some of the village people cautioned, "Many
of our Ojibway people have gone south, and they
have not returned. It is possible that they were
caught by the soldiers and called Dakota and then,
perhaps, killed."

But Oona insisted on going south, and because
she was a Dreamer, the people respected her wishes.
With Oona and A-wa-sa-si-s was his younger
brother, who was nine years old. The small party
followed the Nig-gig-gwa-no-we-si-bi, the Otter Tail
River, south to the place where the forests melted into the prairie lands.

There were white peoples' homesteads here and
there, so the three were very careful and quiet. They
did not want to be seen by the pale strangers. When

they reached what was once the land of the Dakota, they again traveled within the forests.

It was late fall. Beautiful leaves of red, yellow, orange, and brown cushioned the earth beneath the tall trees, and the sun lent a little warmth to the air. The snows had not yet come, but winter was blowing its cold breath, clashing with the warmth. The travelers were quiet as they set their traps. When that work was done, they spent some time in peaceful meditation.

As they began their winding journey homeward, a troop of soldiers suddenly appeared and fired on them. They fled into the barren forests, but more and more soldiers arrived and soon they were surrounded and captured.

The soldiers laughed and joked as they prodded the captives with sticks and the ends of their rifles. Then they tied Little Brother to one end of a rope and a horse to the other. They were going to have Little Brother dragged to death.

When the soldiers hit the horse to make it run, Oona shouted a word and the horse immediately stopped. The soldiers were amazed. Again they hit the horse, and again Oona shouted the word and it stopped. They tried another horse, but each time Oona said the word, the horse would not run. The soldiers let Oona take the rope off Little Brother.

Oona knew it was necessary to make the soldiers realize that they were peaceful Ojibway. She approached them and tried to explain, but the soldiers would not distinguish an Ojibway from a Dakota. Then Oona thought of the birch bark she carried.

She opened her bundle and showed it to them, and one of the soldiers associated the birch bark with the Ojibway. He told his friends not to harm the people.

The three were placed in a tent, with guards to watch over them. Several times during the day the soldiers looked into the tent, and their speaking had a threatening sound to it. The Ojibway did not quite understand the words of the soldiers, but their rude, harsh voices had a touch of anger that could turn to violence. The Ojibway knew they must escape.

That night Oona took her pipe and filled it with kin-nik-a-nik. She smoked and dreamed. Thus she communicated with the Great Being, and she asked for a heavy fog. When she awoke she told the others what they must do.

"We must count the ones put to watch us," said Oona, "and we must count the time between their steps. Then we must rest."

When the dawn came, it was covered by a heavy, heavy fog. The family listened for the tread of the sentries. Then one by one they left the tent, each in the stillness after a sentry had passed.

One by one they followed the river until the first hill was in sight. There each waited. When they were together again, they went into the long prairie grass, for they knew the soldiers would look for them in the forest. They slept by day and journeyed only during the hours of the night-flying bird, the misty morning and the tired twilight hours that had been given to Oona to protect her in times of danger.

They traveled toward the setting sun. Oona said it must be so because of her dream and because the soldiers would expect them to travel east and north, to the Ojibway forest communities.

After two days they came to an earthen lodge. They heard sounds from within—Ojibway chanting. They entered the lodge and found a very old Ojibway man.

He said to Oona, "I have been expecting you. I sent my thoughts to your farm, for my daughter's lodge is nearby. I wish to see her, but because I am as I am, I need help to get there and so I have sent my thoughts."

And indeed the Old One needed help, for his leg had been broken. He could neither hunt nor fish nor make the journey home alone, so he had sent his thoughts to his kinsmen. He knew a Dreamer would catch his thoughts.

That is the way of the Dreamers of the Ojibway. That is why Oona knew she must make the journey south, close to the land of war.

Danger was always near on the journey home, made slow by the needs of the old man. But the twilight and dawn hours were good, and before the snow fell the trapping party and the old man reached home safely.

Times of Change

THE CHILDREN of Oona, E-quay, and Mary were Sa-gwa-de Anishinabe, mixed-bloods, but they were true in the spirit of the Ojibway. Oona had two sons, and each was given the ceremony of the naming. Each received his song and medicine bag according to the old custom. In the way of the Ojibway, Oona's sons were called A-bo-wi-ghi-shi-g (Warm Sky), and Gi-ghi-ki-wa-an-si (Brother). In the way of the white man, they were called Robert and John.

Grandfather said, "Oona, I look at you and I see the goodness of the Ojibway. I believe our ways will survive. Your life today is different from the forest life, but it is good. Your sons have had their namings. The children of E-quay and Mary are on their part of the circle. You have taught the descendants of A-wa-sa-si, just as you promised her you would. There are good Ojibway kinsmen on each side of the churning water."

E-quay's father, Ge-pa-gwa-na-gwa-d, had the lung disease and went deep into the forest. David, when he heard the news, went in search of him and brought him home. Ge-pa-gwa-na-gwa-d left on his journey through the churning waters, but it would

113

be a calm journey, for he had honored all that an Ojibway should. He was mourned in the old Ojibway way. After that Grandfather and Grandmother asked to have a lodge in the woods behind the farm. Oona's heart wept. She knew that they wished to make their journey.

In the third year of Oona's new life, Grandfather and Grandmother made the journey together. They had not been baptized. They were prepared in the old way. In their last resting place on this side of the water they were covered with birch bark, and their tools were buried with them. The mourning lasted a year. They would never be forgotten, for their names were whispered to the si-si-gwa-d.

The farm provided well for Oona's family and yielded gifts for others as well. Much of it was garden, including great fields of corn and potatoes, for these were now the staple food of the Ojibway. This food was never sold. To make money, the family raised wheat and barley and kept milk cows. They never drank milk. It was alien to their taste. The favorite drink of the Ojibway had been raspberry tea. Now when the young raspberry shoots were coiled, tied, and boiled, they were mixed with the green China tea.

Oona and E-quay did the canning with Mary, who came often with her family to the farm. They cooked the vegetables in huge kettles over an open fire out-of-doors. Then they packed the food in Mason jars and steamed it in large oval boilers. They waxed rutabagas and stored them along with carrots and potatoes in root cellars. They put fish in salt brine then dried it in an outdoor oven. This method was quicker than the old way of hanging it on racks above a fire. The children still threshed string beans in the old way, by dancing on them, picking out the beans, and sacking them.

There were always people of the do-daim to help with the farm work. It was they who brought the wild berries and the other forest food. A-wa-sa-si-s taught the children of the farm the new work methods, and Oona told them about the forest ways. She told each child the history and legends of his people so they would learn to respect the past. Her sons were put into the forest for the visions. They were given the drum, the pipe, the kin-nik-a-nik. They sang the Ojibway songs. They learned to offer the first fruits of the harvest, and they learned the way of sharing, for their lodges were always full. They never met the Mi-de-wi-wi-n people or knew their secret ceremonies, but they learned of the ancestors who had belonged. They tipped their hats to the Old Ones and shook their hands to show respect.

Oona's sons attended the white man's school in the big Ojibway village and became skilled in reading and writing and arithmetic. They learned when to reap the grain and the hybrid corn. They learned to draw the milk for market and breed the hens for bigger eggs. They went to the Christian church to read the book and learn new ways which were akin to the ways of the past. The two worlds within them were respected and their hearts were with their Ojibway brothers. They did not yearn for the things that could be counted.

Oona's grandchildren, too, learned the ways of

respect. Because they lived near the big village, they could live at home and go to the government schools. Oona taught them the ways of their people. They too were able to hear the si-si-gwa-d, to remember and teach.

Oona left the farm only to do what was necessary. She helped the older Ojibway with the mourning, which had become a mixture of the old and new. It was now the custom to have a wake and keep vigil with the family. These wakes were held in either the Catholic or Episcopal guild halls. The hymns of the white people were sung but the words were of the Ojibway tongue. The people still put the clothes of the dead into a bundle and gave them to a close friend to distribute among people of another do-daim. But this custom, too, was changed. No longer did the people spend a year in mourning before giving away the clothes and holding a feast. Now everything was done immediately after the funeral.

As the years passed, Oona saw the little villages on the reservation grow into small towns. Greenwood came to have about three hundred people. These people were never rich with material wealth, but they were rich with the culture and customs of the past. But the influence of the white strangers on the Ojibway way of life continued. The time between Oona's fortieth and fiftieth years was full of difficult changes.

Many Ojibway families still lived far from the towns where the schools were. The children could not walk the eight or ten miles each day, so the government built boarding schools for them to stay in. The teachers were the white strangers. Some were good and the others did not care about the children, but they all agreed the Ojibway must change their ways. As Grandfather had predicted many years before, much was lost when the children were made to go to the schools.

In Oona's part of the reservation there were two boarding schools and one mission school. The mission school was run by the nuns who taught the Catholic doctrine and catechism. The children were required to go to church almost daily except when the weather was very bad.

Then came the laws to control the fishing, the hunting, and the trapping, even on the reservation lands. The Ojibway, however, continued to net fish and hunt deer as they had always done. But rarely did they do the trapping.

Like the others, Oona and E-quay still laid nets for the fish and pulled them in early in the morning. But they had to clean, salt, and dry their catch inside their house instead of in the outdoor ovens, so the man who enforced the laws against using nets would not know.

For a time, Oona and her family group practiced the ricing in the old Ojibway way. They chose a ricing leader and respected what he said, and they threshed by dancing on the rice wearing new, soft moccasins. They put the rice to dry in the sun, but they spread it on canvas instead of the birch bark. They continued the custom of blowing the first rice to the east, to the west, to the north, to the south.

But then the white people made laws and regulations for the harvesting of ma-no-min, the precious gift to the Ojibway. These laws set the time for taking the rice, disregarding the wisdom of the ricing leaders who could truly say when the rice was ready. To the Ojibway, the new system was a desecration, for the first rice to ripen was to be offered to the Gitchi Manito and be carried on the wind. For a time the Ojibway had to buy licenses and so pay for what had always been a part of their life.

The children were even farther removed from the traditional harvest. They could never learn the respect for the precious ma-no-min, because they had to attend the boarding schools.

When the white strangers began harvesting the wild rice, many of the Ojibway adopted their methods. They gathered the rice in wooden boats instead of birch-bark canoes, threshed by shaking it in big galvanized drums attached to car motors, and parched it in iron kettles.

The gathering of blueberries was still important to many Ojibway families. They traveled by truck far north of the reservation to pick the berries in galvanized pails. They sold much of their harvest to commercial buyers who came to the blueberry camps. Although they kept some berries for home use, many did not dry them in the old way. Instead, they canned the berries in Mason jars. For as long as Oona lived, she continued drying the berries in the old way, spreading them on sheets of birch bark in the sun. But she also spread them on the tar-paper roofs of the sheds because this method was faster.

Only a few of the old people went to the sugar bush or gathered herbs. In the years after Grandfather and Grandmother were gone, Oona honored their memory by keeping up their practice of gathering the medicine. She stored it in glass jars.

Oona's heart broke many times when she saw the faces of the young ones. Many of the children had swollen necks from infections of the tubercular germ, and they easily caught the diseases of the lungs. The change of diet left them with no way to fight the germs of the strangers who were dominant in the land of the forest and lakes.

It was good that the rulers of the land built hospitals and placed nurses and doctors on the reservations, but even they could not stem the tide of the alien diseases. The government nurses said in tones of disgust, "Soap and water is what is needed. Dirt and disease go together." But soap and water could not replace the diet that had kept the Ojibway people strong. The game and the wild food with its natural strength were not theirs anymore. They had been replaced by the salt pork, bacon, and beans. Later the Ojibway succumbed to a disease of the spirit. They began to drink the aliens' liquors, which helped them forget that they were classed as caricatures in a land that once honored them.

With hunting, fishing, and ricing restricted, more and more Ojibway men went to work in the lumber industry. They needed money to support and feed their families and to buy the things they wanted. There were many logging camps around the reservation, and the big companies that ran them also made the laws. The settlements were supplied by a main camp, called headquarters, which even had its own slaughterhouse. Pigs and cows bought from local farmers were butchered there, and other merchandise and equipment were brought in from the mill towns.

Two camps near White Earth were composed mostly of Ojibway men and boys. They were treated the same as all the other workers. They lived in long rail shacks and ate in a community dining hall. Ojibway women and children sometimes went with their menfolk to the camps. The lumber companies paid some of the women to wash and mend the loggers' clothes.

Life was friendly in the Ojibway camps, and the old customs prevailed. The people shared and helped one another.

The logging season lasted from winter through the spring. In winter the cutting of timber and the skidding of logs were the major operations. Huge logs were towed to a lake on big sleds pulled by three or four teams of horses or oxen. The logs were stacked along the shore until the spring breakup of ice, when they would be driven through four lakes and two rivers to the closest sawmill town. The trip usually took about two months. Indian men and boys, who were adept and very agile, were the best logrollers in the business. They also became very good with the saws. They were of great benefit to the lumber companies, which were glad to employ them.

The logrollers would return from the mill town with supplies for headquarters and the other logging camps. When they got back, there was always a general celebration with square dancing. The Ojibway people learned this alien dance and became very good at it. Then, after the celebration, the families

went back to their reservation homes until the logging season started again, after the wild-rice harvest.

There were many wild-hay meadows in the reservation areas, and just before the rice harvest—in August and early September—Ojibway work crews cut
and dried the hay. The logging companies paid them
on a contract basis to supply this feed for their horses
and oxen.

Around 1910 the big logging companies moved
west and many Ojibway had to find work in smaller
camps. There were fewer jobs and the work was not
as good as before. The lumber companies still fur-
nished the long shacks but no supplies or merchandise. Much of the logrolling was eliminated; instead,
the logs were taken to railroad depots. Lumber was
cut rough and paid for by the cord. If a stand of timber was good, then the cutting was good, and the
weekly wage might be good. Some Ojibway families
clung to this kind of employment. They were fortunate to have it.

These years were times of reflection for Oona.
She could see the lives of the people changing, and
she could see the need for earning money. But to
herself she thought, "I did all the things that my
grandmother and mother taught me to do, such as
making the maple sugar, cutting the birch bark, and
digging the medicine plants. Even in today's world
these things are necessary for us to survive."

Self-sufficiency was more important than ever.
Oona and other women now dug the snake root
every May and June to sell to stores which resold it
to the drug companies for use in patent medicines.
She sold cedar and rush mats, willow and sweet-

grass baskets, and birch-bark containers; she tanned deerskin and made moccasins and beaded bags for sale. Oona learned to knit, crochet, tat, embroider, make rugs and bobbin lace. She was a skillful weaver, as her mother had been. She made bags just like her grandmother had, using yarn instead of the wi-go-b. She sold homemade jam.

In these difficult times, the people of the farm were one with the people of the reservation. A-wa-sa-si-s sank a pump and built a deep well lined with planks that had hooks on them for hanging food. All the neighbors used the well in the summer to store their butter and meat.

Oona helped organize a club called the First Daughters of America. It met twice a month to piece quilts, knit, and do beading or other craftwork. The women talked about gardening and methods of canning. They held square dances to raise money and had free community dinners to which everybody brought and shared food.

During World War I many women knitted socks for the men who left to help fight the war. While others made the upper sock, Oona did the heels and the exacting finishing work. She often thought, "I have learned to do all these things because my grandmother told me to learn from the white people everything that would help, if it was good. The words of the Old Ones were indeed wise."

In the 1930s the lumber operations changed again, this time to making pulpwood. There were many pulp camps near White Earth and even in the reservation forests. Many Ojibway families again were employed, but again the work was not so good. Cutting the trees was a one-man job. After the trees were felled and trimmed, they were measured with a one-hundred-inch "pulp stick" and cut to size. After twenty-five to fifty sticks of rough timber were cut and stacked, the bark was peeled off. Workers earned five cents a stick; their incomes depended on weather conditions, finding a good stand of timber, and the number of working hours – sometimes from sunrise to sunset. And now there were tax deductions but no benefits. The pulp-peeling operations began in May and lasted until the middle of August when the pulp dried out and the peeling became difficult if not impossible.

Ojibway women and children worked at peeling the pulpwood as well as the men. Although the Ojibway were hired at the same rate as others, they sometimes did not receive all that was due them. In many camps the pulp boss and a nearby storekeeper would give credit to the Ojibway families. When the paydays came the money went directly to the storekeeper, who kept most of it for "debts." The people continued to share what they had, however, so they did not always fall into the trap of the boss's and storekeeper's credit system. But it was a transient business, and moving from place to place kept the children out of school.

Then the government built boarding schools hundreds of miles from the Ojibway villages. Each fall the children, five to fifteen years old, were taken to these faraway schools. They returned home only in the summer. The children learned only the new ways: spelling, geography, arithmetic, reading, penmanship, and history—the history of the white people who now ruled in their land.

There were children of many other tribes in these schools, and all were taught to forget their past and beliefs. They could not speak their ancient words, for only English was allowed.

When they returned home in the summer, there was little time to teach them the old ways. They did not hear the legends, for these were told only in the winter. And in the summer the missionaries came in wagons to teach them the "true path."

The two churches in the Ojibway villages— Catholic and Episcopal—became an influence in the Ojibway life. It was in the church guild halls that the sewing circles met and the family dinners were held. There the people gathered for the other Christian practices: the vigils for the dead, and the community Christmas tree and celebration. They went from home to home for prayer meetings. The naming-of-the-child ceremony was never used; instead the person who held the child at baptism became the namer.

These practices were all that the boarding-school children knew about Ojibway life. Those who knew about the old ways were silent. They were never asked to speak.

There were roller skating, bingo, and cards. There were the "old-time dancing" and the roadhouse. The children could hum the songs from the radio but did not know the songs of the drum. Many became wise in the strangers' ways. They played the strangers' games – the baseball, the basketball, and the football – but they never learned the games of the Ojibway.

When these Ojibway children who went to the boarding schools became the young adults and then the older people, they could not teach their own children the old ways. Their children too went to the government boarding schools, and so a cycle began that made the Ojibway forget their past.

They danced the powwow and did the beadwork because these were expected of them by the tourists from the east. They did the planting and the harvesting, the blueberry picking and the ricing, for these were necessary. But they never stood with eyes cast down before the Old Ones to ask about the old ways and the old people. They never offered the first of the harvest. They did not respect the Mi-de-wi-wi-n people. Instead they feared them. They never knew the forest trails and the animal people. They never gathered herbs and medicine or listened to the si-si-gwa-d.

The spirit of the Ojibway was far from the spirit of the beginning.

The Circle

IN 1930 Oona and A-wa-sa-si-s shared the farm with their great-grandson, Ni-sho-ga-bo (Two Standing), his wife, and their four sons. Ni-sho-ga-bo, or Carl, ran the farm. This arrangement made a complete Ojibway family, according to the old custom. Oona and A-wa-sa-si-s were now the Old Ones who taught the practices and told the legends of the do-daim to their great-great-grandchildren.

Two of Ni-sho-ga-bo's sons worked for another farmer seventy miles to the west. It was their duty to drive a herd of cattle seven miles to a water and salt-lick site. Their route followed the edge of a thick forest, with swaying prairie grasses and hayfields along the other side of the trail.

The boys knew every stick, tree, stump, and bush that grew along the cattle trail, so it was with considerable surprise and agitation that one day they came upon a stump standing in a hayfield. A stump where there had never been a stump. As they looked at it, it seemed to be pointing east. As they approached it, it seemed to recede to the east. As they watched it from the trail, a night-flying bird hovered over it.

Then they knew: Oona was sending a message. She wanted them home. The two boys journeyed the seventy miles and found their great-great-grandfather A-wa-sa-si-s very ill. He would soon make the long journey, but first he must clasp the hands of his children and wish them well. Oona with her pipe and kin-nik-a-nik had smoked and dreamed and made it possible.

A-wa-sa-si-s was sixty-nine years old when he died. He was buried in the Christian way. Oona in her grief felt that she would never dream again.

In her late years, Oona never went to Greenwood. The Ojibway who lived there seemed to be a different people. They were not of the forest. They were on the path of the strangers' circle, grasping all the new ways.

She remembered well the last visit she had made to the old, big Ojibway village with Thomas, her fifth great-grandson. There had been many young people and many, many children. As they drove through and around the village, she had looked for familiar faces, and not finding any, she began looking at the young people for resemblances to the old ones she used to know.

A feeling of sadness and loss had come over her, for although these young people were Ojibway, she felt like an outsider. The polite smiles they gave her were those offered to a stranger. The old reservation village that Oona remembered so vividly was a new place with people who seemed much like the white strangers. The people did not say to which do-daim they belonged but instead to which reservation.

There were fine government buildings: a nurse's office and residence, the home of the agent, the school building, and the teachers' houses. Scattered about were the homes of the Ojibway, most of them houses covered with tar paper. There was no plumbing, no electricity; the people lived with kerosene lamps, a water pump, and a house out back.

There was cleanliness within the homes. The floors were bleached white by the lye water. The clothes were boiled and scrubbed. There were braided rugs on the floors, oilcloths on the tables, and curtains on the windows. Little rows of flowers grew outside the doors. There was honesty and doors were left unlocked.

The Ojibway were now a Christian people. They went to the churches, were baptized, and did what was required. The older people who knew the "old Indian ways" could relate them to what was taught in the churches. "Honor thy father and mother," "Love thy neighbor as thyself," "Thou shalt not kill," respect, brotherhood, "Thou shalt not covet thy neighbor's goods" – these were what the Ojibway had always practiced. The Old Ones believed that Christian principles that were similar to the old ways could help the Ojibway people.

Oona, in her eightieth year, sat rocking and remembering the years before. She remembered the feeling of belonging to the past and how it was when there were only Ojibway in the land. She remembered the blueberries simmering in the muk-kuk. She recalled the taste of popped ma-no-min mixed with maple sugar and the aroma of burning cedar in her grandmother's lodge.

She thought of the Old Ones and the old Ojib-way names: On-da-bi-tung (Up Step-By-Step), A-bo-wi-ghi-shi-g (Warm Sky), Me-ow-ga-bo (Outstand-ing). She thought of A-wa-sa-si, Mother, On-da-g, and E-quay. She remembered the old families very well, and she could still picture their faces. She thought of the old lodges and the thick forests, and her thoughts returned to the many times she had moved to reach this, her final home.

Oona thought about her children, the grand-children, and the many great-grandchildren and great-great-grandchildren. They had all been taught the Ojibway beliefs, but would they teach the children yet to come?

"My children and grandchildren are doing well in the way of the white strangers," thought Oona. "They are farmers, they are teachers, and they work in the factories that make the many new tools — even the airplanes that crowd the birds from the sky. And they are with honor, for they have fought in the white man's wars. Because of this, part of my dust lies in the foreign lands.

"My mother said to me," thought Oona, "that our dust cannot be erased from the earth of our land. Let this be true also for my children who lie in the for-eign lands, for I have buried the drums that were a part of their lives."

Oona thought about the Ojibway children. It had been a long, long time since a child had come to hear the legends and the stories of the old life.

'Maybe they do not care," thought Oona. "If this is so, then our history will be lost."

Oona rocked and rocked and she gazed out at the

trees. She heard the si-si-gwa-d, the murmuring that the trees make, and it seemed their hearts were crying, too.

There was a knock, and Oona turned and saw a small girl in the doorway. The child stood with eyes cast down just as Oona had stood before her grandmother. Oona said, "Come in, my child, and speak if you wish to do so."

The child said, "My name is Mary in the English way, but in the language of our people, I am called A-wa-sa-si."

"And what is it you wish, my child?" asked Oona.

"I should like," said the child, "to hear the stories of our people."

Oona felt a joy in her spirit and a light on her face. She knew that the Ojibway ways would forever be known in future years.

"My name is Ni-bo-wi-se-gwe," said Oona, "and I shall tell you of our people. . . ."

Mi-i-yu

GLOSSARY

The Ojibway words in the text are the author's phonetic transcriptions of the spoken language. English vowels take the following sounds:

a - ah	i - ee
e - ay	o - oh

SPELLING	MEANING
A-bo-wi-ghi-shi-g	Warm Sky
A-bwa-na-g	Dakota (Minnesota River)
A-ki-wa-a-si	Old Man
A-na-gwa-d	Cloud
A-ni-mi-ki	Thunder
Anishinabe	Person
A-sa-bi-ig-go-na-ya	People of Nettle Fibers
A-wa-sa-si	Bullhead
A-wa-sa-si-s	Little Fisher
Ba-ca-ne-ge	Isolation lodge
Ba-ghi-gi-ge-win	Gift Dance
Bi-mi-wi-t-gi-ga-n	Travois
Bis-in-d-an	Listen
Che-ro-ki	Cherokee

SPELLING	MEANING
Chi-o-ni-ga-mig	Big Lake (Lake Superior)
Chi-si-bi	Big River (Mississippi)
Do-daim	Clan, totem
E-quay	Lady
Ga-ga-yo-sh-ko-ons-i-ca	Place where small gulls live
Ga-w-in Mi-shi	Not yet
Ge-pa-gwa-na-gwa-d	Thick Cloud
Gi-ghi-ki-wa-an-si	Brother
Gitchi Manito	Great Spirit
Kin-nik-a-nik	Red willow tobacco
Ki-we-di-n	North Wind
Ma-da-min	Corn
Ma-gi-ghi-shi-g	Starting Sky
Ma-i-ga-n	Wolf
Ma-no-min	Wild rice
Ma-s-gi-go-ba-go-n	Swamp leaves
Me-ow-ga-bo	Outstanding
Mi-de-wi-wi-n	Grand Medicine People
Mi-go-s	Needle, awl
Mi-i-yu	That's all
Mi-n-di-mo-ye	Old Lady
Mi-s-gwa-ghi	Fox
Mo-wi-ga-n	Mohegan
Muk-kuk	Container
Muk-kuk-ko-ons-sug	Containers
Muk-kwa	Bear
Ni-bo-wi-se-gwe	Night Flying Woman
Nig-gig-gwa-no-we-si-bi	Otter Tail River
Ni-gi	Friend

SPELLING	MEANING
Ni-shi-ma	My younger kin
Ni-sho-ga-bo	Two Standing
Nuco	Term of endearment
O-bi-mi-wi-i-to-n	Carrying Place (Grand Portage)
O-bo-da-wa-da-mi-g	Build-Fire People (Potawatomi)
O-da-wa	Ottawa
O-ge-ma	Leader
O-Gitchi Da	Talk Dance
O-ma-no-ma-ni-g	Wild Rice People (Menominee)
On-da-bi-tung	Up Step-By-Step
On-da-g	Crow
On-da-g-o-ba-go-sin	Peppermint
Sa-gwa-de Anishinabe	Mixed-bloods
Shi-n-go-b	Trees
Si-si-gwa-d	Sounds trees make
Si-s-sa-ba-gwa-d	Maple sugar
Wa-bo-os	Rabbit
Wa-wi-e-cu-mig-go-gwe	Round Earth
Wi-go-b	Forest string
Wi-ni-bo-sho	Mythical hero
Wi-ni-shi-ba-go-sin	Evergreen